TENS

I never did like football much. I was ten before I knew what it was. Cricket was my game, fast bowler. Not so good at hitting the ball with a bat, but I could hit a batsman's middle wicket, no problem. In my first inter-school match I got ten wickets. Couldn't see what the fuss was about concerning football.

Even after I heard my late uncle Sam say to my father one July afternoon, "Frank, it's that Hurst! He's got another!" I just wasn't impressed. I was busy that afternoon, writing another story. Much more interesting.

England didn't win the World Cup until after I was ten. Big deal. It took me another few years to even watch a footie match on the telly. West Bromwich Albion v Everton at the Hawthorns. Everton smashed West Brom that day and I watched spellbound as Alan Ball helped himself to four goals, Everton winning by six goals to two. I was hooked and have had a little more than a soft spot for the Toffees ever since that day, even though I'm geographically a Mancunian. Only weeks later, I had my first feelings of heartache and bitterness when West Brom got their revenge against 'my' team - in the 1968 Cup Final of all matches.

What has this to do with the number 10 shirt? Nothing, really, but, as any Everton fan will know, in those days their number 10 was John Hurst (no relation to the above). But he was defender and had no right to wear that number. It was a forwards' number, or, failing that, a midfielders. Someone with flair, with the skill to turn a game. Law was 10 for Manchester United, and later Hoddle was 10 for Spurs. People like that.

All his international career, Pelé was the number 10 for the boys from Brazil. He wore 10 in 1958, aged seventeen, in the World Cup Final and he was still wearing it twelve years later, again in a World Cup Final. He was the greatest footballer the world has seen, before or since, ever. Period. Better than Puskas, better than Georgie, better than Eusabio, just better than anyone. After I'd seen the light and began playing football, I was the number 10. I had flair, I had skill, I was a forward and I scored goals. I was as good as Pele! When I played for the school team - number 10. When I moved into the local Sunday League a year later - number 10. I still have that very shirt - 10. My family lived at number 10. Everything I did, pointed to number 10. Even my birthdate . . . take 5 off 15 and you have - 10. If you add the last two numbers of the year I was born - 1955 - you have 10. A magical number. 10. Precise. 10. Neat. 10. Just say it . . .

Nowadays, it seems that every team's best player wears 10. Maybe Alan Shearer would argue with that, but his first game for his country, against France at Wembley in 1992, he wore what was then Gary Lineker's shirt. 10. And he scored. Geoff Hurst, our hat-trick hero of that glorious '66 team - 10. Maradona, love him or hate him, in his prime the best in the world - 10. When Dennis Bergkamp moved from Inter to Arsenal, he demanded he wore what was then Paul Merson's shirt - 10. Zico, Rivelino, Kempes, Gullit. 10.

It's a magical number.

For magical players.

For a magical game.

10 TENS
A Britespot Publication

First Published in Great Britain by
Britespot Publishing Solutions Limited
Chester Road, Cradley Heath, West Midlands B64 6AB

May 2002

ISBN 1 904103 14 6

Cover design and layout
© Britespot Publishing Solutions Limited

Printed and bound in Great Britain by
Cradley Print Limited, Chester Road, Cradley Heath, West Midlands B64 6AB

Acknowledgments
As the author, I would like to thank Neil Boardman for the tip off and Ian Nannestad for assisting me with the clarification of the facts and figures contained in this book. I would also like to thank Jen Little at Empics and Nicholas at Allsport for supplying the photographs and of course, there is a special thank you to Roger Marshall and Paul Burns at Britespot Publishing for all their help and support in making this project a dream come true.

This book is dedicated in its entirety to my late father, Francis William Fleming, who told me I could wear my number ten shirt with pride.

CONTENTS

PELÉ
PERFECTION

PELÉ
BRAZIL

A star of four World Cup final tournaments, Pelé was probably the most complete player in the history of football. He was born at Tres Coraçoes in the state of Minas Gerais, Brazil on 23 October 1940 under the name of Edson Arantes do Nascimento. His father had played the game professionally and the youngster showed great talent from an early age, first being spotted by the former Brazilian international player Waldemar de Brito. At the age of 15 he signed for Santos and shortly before his 16th birthday he made his senior debut, scoring against Corinthians. He quickly shot to fame and went on to make his debut for Brazil in the first leg of the Copa Roca tie against Argentina in July 1957 when he was used as a second half substitute, but although he scored his team went down to a 2-1 defeat. He added another in the second leg as the Brazilians won 2-0 to take the trophy 3-2 on aggregate.

Despite a troublesome knee injury he made the national squad for the 1958 World Cup finals in Sweden and it was here that he established himself as a key figure in the world game. The tournament will always be remembered for the grace and beauty lent to it by the irrepressible South Americans, although it would be wrong to assume that Pelé was the only star in the team for the likes of Garrincha, Zagallo and Vava all played their part too. Brazil team played a bold and innovative formation: 4-2-4. After their success many teams attempted to emulate them using the system, but none were able to achieve the same devastating effect. Simply put, Brazil did not seem to know the meaning of defence. Their entire game was built around attacking and winning. If their defence let in three goals and they scored four, what was the problem? That said, it must be noted that they almost missed qualification. Faced with a two-leg encounter with Peru they were held to a 1-1 draw in Lima but just a single goal was enough to win the return match in Rio and book their trip to Stockholm. Although only 5ft 8in tall, Pelé could leap like a high jumper and sprint better than most 100 metre runners of his time. Injury kept him out of the first two group games against Austria (won 3-0) and England (0-0) and it was only in the third game against the Soviet Union that he appeared in the line-up. His quick thinking and perfect passing ability belied his tender age and he went on to score the only goal of the game in the quarter-final against

Sweden 1958. The victorious Brazil team with the trophy: (back row, L-R) Coach Vicente Feola, Djalmar Santos, Zito, Bellini, Nilton Santos, Orlando, Gilmar (front row, L-R) Garrincha, Didi, Pelé, Vava, Mario Zagalo, trainer.

Wales. The defenders hesitated, Pelé fired in a shot from six yards and the ball deflected off full back Williams and landed in the net. He later described the goal as the most important of his career. The Brazilians crushed France 5-2 in the semi-final. Just Fontaine, still the only man to score 13 goals in one tournament and the first to score against Brazil in the 1958 finals, tormented the South Americans' defence throughout the game but only found the net once. Brazil led 2-1 at half time, the scorers

Sweden 1958. Pelé watches French goalkeeper Claude Abbes pounce on the ball in the semi-final game.

being Vava and Didi, but the second half belonged to Pelé who hit a hat-trick in just over 20 minutes. As the goals went in, the quality of each surpassed the other. The first was a simple tap in as the French 'keeper dropped the ball at his feet. The second was a well taken half-chance from the edge of the six-yard box. The third was a brilliant effort finished with a perfect volley from the edge of the penalty area. The first half had been close, but the Brazilians stepped up their game several gears and France were unable to quell the onslaught, despite scoring a second seven minutes from full time. Then it was on to the final at the Rasunda Stadium in Solna, Stockholm and an encounter with the host nation. The Swedes produced a major shock by taking a fourth minute lead but the response was emphatic. Five minutes later Garrincha centred for Vava to level the scores and on the half hour Garrincha again swept passed the Swedish defence and crossed for Vava to net his second. The scores remained unaltered at half time. When the teams reappeared it was soon all over as a contest. Ten minutes after the re-start Pelé trapped the ball on his chest and flicked the ball brilliantly over a Swedish defender's head before volleying home. Zagallo then scored a fourth. Sweden added a second, but the game was passing them by and Brazil were clearly in control. Almost on full time, Pelé began a move down the Swedish left flank with a sweet back heel pass to Zagallo and the 17-year-old Pelé headed his second and his country's fifth of the game. After six attempts, including the

Sweden 1958. Pelé (left) steers the ball past France goalkeeper Claude Abbes to score Brazil's third goal in the semi final game

heartbreaking failure to beat Uruguay in the Maracana Stadium in 1950, Brazil had at last won the World Cup and this victory was the first time a team had won the tournament on a continent other than their own. Pelé, at the time the youngest ever player to compete in the World Cup finals, ended the game in tears. He finished the tournament as joint-second leading goal-scorer, behind Fontaine, with six goals and was one of only two men to score a hat-trick in these finals.

Brazil were again favourites to win the trophy in Chile four years later. This time they employed a slightly more disciplined formation, 4-3-3, a system that seemed to restrict the free-flowing football that the world adored. They opened their campaign with a 2-0 win over Mexico. The Mexicans were tough opponents and Pelé and his colleagues felt the full force of some questionable tackling. The first half was a frustrating one for Brazil and ended goalless. Zagallo scored after 56 minutes to give his team a deserved lead and 18 minutes from time Pelé netted one of the greatest goals of his career, using his fantastic strength to burst through the opposition defence and smash the ball home. In

Chile 1962. Pelé in his team blazer at a photo call.

Mexico 1970. Brazil World Cup Team. (Back Row L-R) Carlos Alberto, Brito, Wilson Piazza, Felix, Clodoaldo, Everaldo, unknown. (Front Row L-R) Jairzinho, Roberto Rivelino, Tostao, Pelé, Paulo Cesar

the second group match against Czechoslovakia three days later the South Americans were held at bay despite continual pressure. However Pelé's luck ran out when he suffered a pulled hamstring and he left the field for treatment before eventually returning as a passenger for the remainder of the game. The injury was so serious that he played no further part in the tournament. His replacement for the final group game against Spain another rising star, Amarildo. The youngster came in and scored two goals as Brazil advanced menacingly into the quarter-finals. Their next opponents were England, coached by Walter Winterbottom. Despite including the talents of Bobby Charlton and Jimmy Greaves they were pushed aside 3-1, Garrincha scoring twice and having a brilliant game. The hosts Chile were crushed 4-2 in the semi final, Garrincha, the player of the tournament, again scoring two goals and Brazil were in the final once more where they were due to meet Czechoslovakia for a second time. Once again they went behind to an early goal, but within two minutes they were level, Amarildo scoring from a seemingly impossible angle. Zito and Vava added further goals and the trophy was destined for Rio once more.

1966 and England loomed. Could the Brazilians capture a third successive World Cup in the land where the game was born? The squad was

beginning to age, although Pelé was still only 25 and a few youngsters such as 16-year-old Edu (who did not make an appearance) Jairzinho, Tostao (both 20) and the brilliant midfielder Gerson (24) made the journey to Europe. The first game against Bulgaria proved a difficult obstacle and they refused to allow themselves to be overrun. Sadly, the method they used to thwart the South Americans was literally to stop them from playing. Pelé had a running battle with defender Zhekov. Both players were guilty of intimidation and foul play, yet one has to side with Pelé and say that he was only giving as good as he got. Most of the confrontation happened off the ball and out of sight of the referee. Pelé still managed to score the opening goal, which was also the first goal of the competition. After 15 minutes he struck a free kick from just outside the penalty area and the Bulgarian 'keeper Naidenov could only watch as the ball curled around him. He thus became the first man to score in three successive tournaments. However, injury prevented him from appearing in the second group match and Brazil went down 3-1 to Hungary. It was their first defeat in the World Cup finals since 1954 when they had also been defeated by the Hungarians. Nine changes were made to the line-up for the final group game against Portugal at Goodison Park, Pelé being restored to the team although clearly unfit. Once again he was on the receiving end of some rough treatment and was reduced to the role of an ineffective passenger after only 30 minutes. After this he vowed that he would never play World Cup football again, saying, "I don't want to end up as an invalid."

Fortunately for Brazil he had changed his mind by 1970 and decided to compete in the Mexico World Cup. The South Americans were favourites to win the tournament for a third time. Should they achieve this staggering feat in such a short period, only 12 years after their first victory, the gleaming Jules Rimet Trophy would be theirs to keep forever. Mario Zagallo, one of the stars of the 1958 and 1962 teams, was now head coach. This time Pelé showed another side of his game - he was tougher, even meaner than before. He made the world look up to him again and at 29 he was a more mature player than ever before. Brazil coasted through their qualifying games with a 100 per cent record,

winning all six of their games, scoring 23 goals and conceding only two. Tostao, now a regular in the team, was top scorer with nine goals. New players had been drafted into the squad: skipper Carlos Alberto, an attacking right back with amazing speed and a powerful shot, defenders Clodoaldo and Brito, both tough competitors, and midfielder Roberto Rivelino. Their first opponents were Czechoslovakia, the country they had beaten in the 1962 final. Again the Brazilian defence left a lot to be desired and they went a goal down after only 11 minutes, Rivelino equalising from a curving free kick some 13 minutes later. Pelé then almost scored with an audacious shot from his own half after noticing that the Czech goalkeeper Viktor was standing far off his line. Unfortunately the ball just dropped the wrong side of the post otherwise it would have ranked as one of the greatest ever goals scored in the history of the finals. Pelé then scored a magnificent effort in the 59th minute. Taking a long, searching pass from Gerson on his

Mexico 1970. Pelé (left) celebrates after scoring the opening goal in the final against Italy. Brazil went onto win the match 4-1.

chest, he drew the goalkeeper before sending a screaming shot into the net. He thus became the first man to score in four consecutive World Cup finals. Winger Jairzinho scored two more before the game ended. Brazil were on their way. The next match against England was believed by many to be a dress rehearsal for the final itself. The holders were certainly a match for the Brazilians and were unlucky to lose the game. In the first half the speedy Jairzinho rounded full back Terry Cooper and sent a tantalising cross into the England penalty area. Pelé leapt to get on the end of it. His near-perfect bullet header, moving down and into the corner of goalkeeper Gordon Banks' net, seemed destined for a goal. Banks made the save of the World Cup. Diving to his right, he somehow scooped the ball up and over the crossbar. The first half ended goalless. England were clearly a match for the South Americans and skipper Bobby Moore was

having the game of his life. Several scoring chances were missed before Jairzinho moved on to a defence-splitting pass from Pelé to score the only goal of the game. Their final group match was against the bruisers of Romania. Despite fierce treatment, Pelé scored the opening goal from a free kick after 19 minutes and later scored the third after Jairzinho had netted from close range. The 3-2 score line flattered the Europeans, but Brazil were through to the quarter-final. Here they came across old rivals Peru, managed by their former team-mate Didi. The match was one of the most exciting of the tournament, and although Pelé failed to get on the score sheet he played a magnificent part in his country's 4-2 win. They faced South American opposition again in the semi-final in the form of Uruguay, the winners of the first competition back in 1930, and also winners in 1950. On that occasion the Uruguayans had beaten hosts Brazil

Mexico 1970. That save! England's Gordon Banks makes arguably the greatest save of all time, keeping out a point blank bullet header from Pelé in the Group 3 match at Jalisco Stadium, Guadalajara.

Mexico 1970. Pelé takes to the pitch surrounded by photographers in the World Cup Final against Italy.

at the Maracana Stadium in Rio in the deciding match of the tournament. Naturally, Uruguay thought their team would win the 1970 competition and become the first country to win the Jules Rimet Trophy three times. Pelé and his team-mates had other ideas. Brazil insisted on scaring themselves and their fans by going a goal behind yet again. In the first half Pelé dummied the goalkeeper, allowing the ball to run free while he ran around the keeper and back for the ball. He kicked it as he fell only to see it clip the wrong side of the post. Another 'almost' wonder goal. He failed to score but had a hand in two of the Brazilian goals as they marched on to the final for the third time in four tournaments. Their opponents were Italy, who had also won the tournament on two previous occasions, and so whoever won the match would also retain the trophy. Pelé again showed his class by out jumping the six foot Italian defender Facchetti to score the opening goal. It was Brazil's 100th World Cup goal, and also meant that Pelé joined his fellow countryman Vava as the only players to score in two World Cup final matches. Italy equalised through Roberto Boninsegna from a needless defensive mistake, leaving the half time score at 1-1. After the break Gerson stamped his mark on the game, controlling the midfield before scoring with a fierce left-foot drive that screamed past Italian 'keeper Albertosi. The Brazilians overran the disciplined Italians with

some breathtaking football. Their third came when Pelé headed down a cross for Jairzinho to shoot home and so become the only player to score in every match in a final tournament. The South Americans were in total command and four minutes from time Pelé squared a pass to his captain Carlos Alberto who hammered in the fourth. This final goal typified Brazilian power and style. The move involved nine passes, both long and short, instant control by all involved, a tricky, mazy dribble and a swift, surgical finish. The ghost of 1966 was now buried. This side still stands as probably the best team that ever played in a World Cup final. When asked, Pelé himself had no illusions regarding the differences between the Brazilian teams of 1958 and 1970. The 1970 side was more of a team, he said, more of a balanced unit, while the 1958 squad had greater individuals.

When the great man announced that he would not be making a fifth appearance in the finals of 1974, 40 million Brazilians watched a government-sponsored television programme entitled 'Come Back Pelé'. The final statistics show that he scored 77 goals in 91 appearances for Brazil over 14 years and four World Cups. In total, Pelé scored over 1,200 senior goals in 1,363 senior appearances for club and country. At club level he was a member of the Santos team that won the World Club Championship in

Pelé bids farewell to the 75,000 strong crowd in his final game for New York Cosmos against Santos.

1962 and 1963, the Copa Libertadores twice (1961, 1962), the Brazilian Cup on five consecutive occasions (1961 to 1965) and the Sao Paulo state championship nine times between 1956 and 1973. He played his final game for Santos in 1974. His retirement lasted all of one year after he was persuaded to play in the North American Soccer League, pulling on the number 10 shirt (what else?) of the New York Cosmos in a $4 million deal. In 1976, Pelé played for Team America against England in the United States Bi-Centennial celebrations. He played for Cosmos until 1977 and ended his career fittingly in front of a 75,000 crowd, ironically against his old team Santos when he featured for both sides during the game. Pelé was and is, undisputedly, the greatest player to have graced the game. You will hear reasoned arguments that such players as George Best might have been better, Best was undoubtedly a great footballer, but he never achieved success on the same level as Pelé. Pelé is now one of the greatest ambassadors for the game of football and it was he who coined the phrase 'The Beautiful Game.' Pelé got it right, both on and off the field.

HURST
HAT-TRICK HERO

GEOFF HURST

ENGLAND

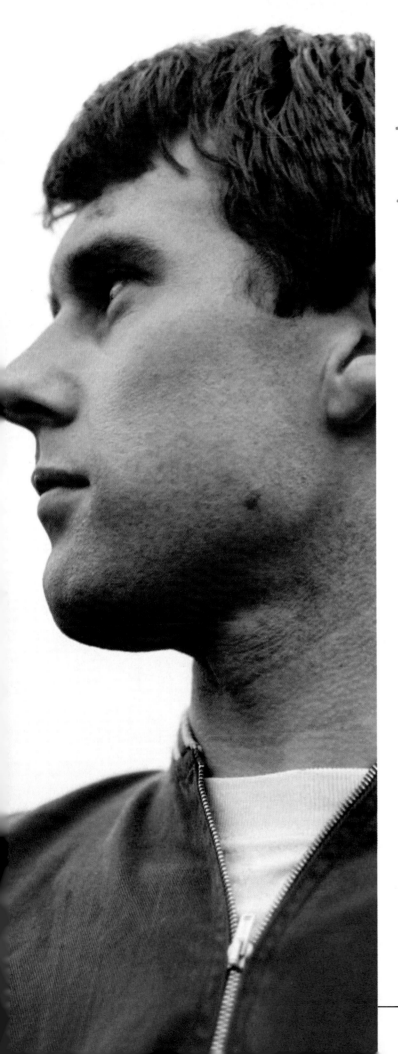

Born in Ashton-under-Lyne, Lancashire in 1941, Geoff Hurst played over 400 games for West Ham United between 1959 and 1972 scoring 180 goals before moving on to Stoke City. A talented youngster who represented England at youth-team level, he achieved wider fame after scoring one of the Hammers' goals in their 3-2 victory over Preston North End in the 1964 FA Cup final. The following year he helped the club lift the European Cup Winners' Cup, again at Wembley, beating Munich 1860 2-0. A year later, Hurst completed a remarkable hat-trick of Wembley appearances when he was a vital member of the England team that won the eighth World Cup tournament. He had made his full international debut only five months before that glorious July day, ironically against West Germany and, yet again, at Wembley.

30 July 1966 was England's finest footballing hour as Alf Ramsey's men, led by Bobby Moore, sank West Germany 4 goals to 2 in extra time. Hurst came into the England team through the back door after Jimmy Greaves picked up an ankle injury in the final group game against France. Many thought that Greaves was fit enough for selection for the quarter-final against Argentina but Hurst took his place. The South Americans, despite being a talented side, began the game with some vicious tackling and their influential captain and midfielder Rattin was sent off after only 36 minutes. In the 78th minute Geoff Hurst scored with a glancing header from a left-wing cross delivered by his West Ham team-mate Martin Peters. That strike was the only goal and indeed the only high point of a bad-tempered game. Hurst himself was lucky not to have been sent off for a bad tackle on an Argentinian shortly after Rattin left the field. At the final whistle, Alf Ramsey came onto the pitch and stopped the England players swapping their shirts with the South Americans. Ramsey would later refer to the Argentinian players as "animals". He subsequently withdrew the statement under pressure from the FA, but the damage had been done. Bad feeling and unfortunate remarks aside, England were in the semi-finals and were finding their form. On 26 July they faced the mighty Portugal whose main threat was provided by Eusebio, who was already leading scorer in the tournament with seven goals and probably second only to Pelé as the greatest footballer in the world at that time. He had single-handedly demolished tiny North Korea in the quarter-final

England 1966. Hurst's perfectly placed header from Bobby Moore's free kick thunders into the West Germany net for Englands equaliser in the 18th minute of the 1966 final.

match, scoring 4 goals in Portugal's 5-3 win, after the Koreans had caused a major sensation by leading 3-0 midway through the opening half. Both England and Portugal were committed to playing football from the first whistle in their semi-final encounter. Much media hype surrounded Eusebio and his possible confrontation with England's tigerish midfield

England 1966. Geoff Hurst slams his shot against the underside of the bar in extra time. Thanks to Tofik Bakhramov, the Russian linesman, the referee awarded England's third and Hurst's second goal. People still question - Did the ball cross the line?

stopper Nobby Stiles. Stiles produced possibly his greatest performance in an England shirt, dominating the strong and pacy Portuguese striker. Although he did not score, Hurst was involved in Bobby Charlton's second goal, laying the ball back for the Manchester United star to shoot home from just inside the penalty area.

After going two goals up by the 79th minute, England played the last eight minutes with their hearts in their mouths. Eusebio pulled one back from the penalty spot and Stiles stopped a Simoes shot in front of goal. For all the Portuguese pressure, England held out and were in their first World Cup final. Everybody, including

England 1966. No doubt about Hurst's hat-trick and Englands fourth. Bobby Moore's 60 yard pass found Hurst free in the Germany half and the West Ham striker did the rest. Wolfgang Overath can only look on in despair.

England 1966. West Germany and England pause for the National Anthems before kicking off the 1966 World Cup final at the Empire Stadium, Wembley.

Hurst, expected a now fit Jimmy Greaves to return for the final against West Germany. Alf Ramsey had other ideas. Instead Greaves watched from the stands as the man who had replaced him, Geoff Hurst, took most of the glory. The 1966 World Cup final was the 200th game to be played in the finals since they had begun back in 1930. Both sides were unchanged from their semi-final successes. The Germans went ahead after 12 minutes when left back Ray Wilson failed to head the ball away from his penalty area. Haller moved onto the awkwardly bouncing ball, mishit his shot and watched in glee as it trickled past England's bewildered goalkeeper, Gordon Banks. England were level only six minutes later, when Overath tripped Bobby Moore just outside the German penalty box. Moore grabbed the ball and was on his feet in seconds, the Germans still organising their defence. Spotting his club colleague Hurst running across the German six-yard box unmarked and screaming for the ball, he sent in a perfectly flighted ball and the striker nodded home past the German 'keeper Tilkowski. 1-1. The game was evenly balanced until the 78th minute when Martin Peters, the third West Ham player in the team, shot England into the lead from close range, running onto a deflected shot from Hurst. Victory looked certain. The Germans looked defeated. However in the dying seconds centre half Jack Charlton was judged to have pushed over the veteran German centre forward

Uve Seeler and the referee awarded Germany a free-kick on the edge of the penalty area. They took it quickly. The ball flashed across the front of the England goal and Germany's Weber slid the ball past Banks' despairing dive. Despite Bobby Moore's protests for handball the 90 minutes of normal time ended 2-2. Ramsey walked onto the pitch before extra time began. His words will never be known for certain, but one of the players later said it was along the lines of, "You've won it once. Now go and do it again." England responded. Alan Ball, just 21, ran down the right wing onto a pin point pass from Nobby Stiles and sent a low cross to the waiting Hurst only six yards from the German goal. Hurst swivelled his body and sent a blistering right-foot shot toward the goal. What happened next is still a matter of great controversy and debate. The ball flew past the German 'keeper struck the underside of the crossbar, dropped down and bounced back into play. German defender Weber, with England's Roger Hunt in close attendance, cleared the ball as it bounced up from the goal line. Hunt was ecstatic and turned with arms raised. He was convinced that the ball had crossed the line. Weber was just as convinced that it hadn't. Hurst, lying on his back following his shot, couldn't be sure. Weber waved his hands, gesturing "No!" Hunt tried to explain to the referee that the ball had crossed the line and the goal should stand. The referee approached his Russian linesman, Tofik

England 1966. Geoff Hurst supports his captain with Ray Wilson as Bobby Moore shows off the Jules Rimet trophy at Wembley during Englands finest sporting hour.

Bakhramov, who signalled that the ball had, indeed, crossed the line and that the goal should stand. 3-2. Today, almost 40 years later, the debate still rages. None of the films and still photos of the incident prove one way or the other what really happened. It is impossible to

England 1966. England team group: Back row (l to r) Harold Shepherdson, Nobby Stiles, Roger Hunt, Gordon Banks, Jack Charlton, George Cohen, Ray Wilson, Sir Alf Ramsey. Front row, (l to r) Martin Peters, Geoff Hurst, Bobby Moore, Alan Ball, Bobby Charlton.

England 1966. Another view of one of the most controversial goals ever scored in the World Cup finals. We will probably never know if the whole of the ball crossed the line.

tell. As the final whistle approached with the referee waving the players to play on, Bobby Moore received the ball in his own penalty area. Jack Charlton and other players were screaming at him to clear it. Anywhere would do, the further the better. The impeccable Moore would have none of it. Looking up, he saw Hurst waving for the ball just inside the German half. He sent a smooth pass over German heads to Hurst who gathered the ball and set off for the German goal. He looked exhausted. As he approached the penalty box, Overath was almost on him, but he smashed the ball, left-footed into the roof of Tilkowski's net putting the result beyond all doubt. The referee blew his whistle and England were champions of the world. Geoff Hurst had become the only player to date to score a hat-trick in a World Cup final.

The 1970 World Cup in Mexico presented the competing nations with new problems – mainly heat and altitude. Although the climate suited the South Americans, the European teams were undaunted and still had a good deal to offer the tournament, not least an England side qualifying as holders and very capable of becoming the first European side to win the World Cup on South American soil. They were favourites after Brazil to lift the trophy. The backbone of the 1966 side was still in place; Banks in goal; Captain Bobby Moore in the centre of defence, and now

playing at his peak, Bobby Charlton running the midfield and Hurst up front with a new striking partner, Manchester City's Francis Lee. England had a stronger squad than the one that had lifted the Jules Rimet Trophy four years earlier. Ramsey said before they left for Mexico that England were "going to be champions a second time." Despite a more negative 4-4-2 formation they still looked to be a formidable team. The first group game against a tough Romanian side was a disappointing encounter. Romanian defender Mocanu was responsible for an injury to full back Keith Newton that kept the England player out of the next fixture. Hurst scored the only goal of the game in the 65th minute. Drawing the goalkeeper off his line, he netted with a low left-foot shot from an acute angle. On 7 June England faced Brazil in their second group match in the Jalisco Stadium in Guadalajara. The Mexican public, having taken the Brazilians to their hearts, kept the England players awake all the previous night by chanting and honking car horns outside the team hotel. Despite a sleepless night they were clearly a match for Pelé and his colleagues and the game was widely seen as a warm-up for the final. England went close in the opening minutes when an unmarked Francis Lee almost netted with a diving header. Half time arrived with no score from either side but brought cool sanctuary from the relentless heat of a 100 degrees temperature. However, when the England players took the field after the break the Brazilians were nowhere in sight. England were kept hanging around for a full five minutes in the glaring heat in what must have been the most blatant act of professionalism in the tournament. Such an incident can only serve to underline the high regard the Brazilians held for their opponents. In the 59th minute, following some wizardry from Tostao and Pelé, Jairzinho blasted the ball past Gordon Banks and that proved to be the only goal of the game. England won their final group tie against Czechoslovakia, again by 1-0, the goal coming from debutant Leeds United striker Allan Clarke who was playing instead of Hurst. England qualified for the quarter-finals by finishing second in their group and once again faced their old rivals West Germany. Before the game England number one goalkeeper Gordon Banks went down with food poisoning and his place was taken by Peter Bonetti. England chose to wear their famous red shirts and the psychological ploy seemed to have worked as they stormed into a two goal lead after 50 minutes through Alan Mullery and Martin Peters. The tie looked over. Then the West German coach Helmut Schön made a tactical substitution that changed the destiny of the game. Franz Beckenbauer pulled a goal back, firing a low shot past Bonetti. Ramsey, still believing the match won, pulled off Bobby Charlton, replacing him with Colin Bell. Then disaster. Uwe Seeler, playing in his fourth and final World Cup, scored the equaliser with a glancing back header. The game moved into extra time. Hurst, after a quiet game, thought he'd scored in the second period, but the goal was disallowed. Then, minutes later, Gerd Müller, 'der Bomber', scored West Germany's winning goal as they avenged their defeat in the final at Wembley four years previously. England's World Cup dream was over. It would be 12 long years before they would again play in the finals.

England 1966. Geoff Hurst follows captain Bobby Moore who is about to proudly receive the World Cup from Her Majesty the Queen.

England 1966. Geoff Hurst Bobby Moore and Martin Peters who played together at West Ham United as well as play a major part in the events at Wembley on that memorable day.

Geoff Hurst played a total of 49 games for England (his final game was against West Germany!) and scored 24 goals, concluding a distinguished player career at West Bromwich Albion. Attempts at management with Chelsea and Telford United proved unsuccessful, although he later became an assistant to Ron Greenwood when the former West Ham manager took over as England team boss in 1977. Hurst now runs his own business with another member of the 1966 squad, Martin Peters.

MARADONA
LA MANOS DÉ DIOS

DIEGO MARADONA

ARGENTINA

Rightly called the most gifted and controversial player of his generation, Diego Armando Maradona was born on 30 October 1960. The fifth of eight children, he grew up in a poor area of Buenos Aires and it was here amidst poverty and desperation, that he honed his dreams and footballing skills. Interviewed at the age of 12, he said that his greatest ambition was to play in and win the World Cup final. He first played for the boys' team of the Argentinos Juniors club and he went on to make his senior debut for them at the age of 15. A year later he won his first cap for Argentina against Hungary, playing his part in a 2-1 win. He only came on a substitute in the second half, the crowd were already chanting his name and he later recalled it as one of the highlights of his career. Although only five foot five, he was very powerfully built, his small stature and exceptional pace making his balance perfect. These attributes, combined with excellent close control of the ball whilst running at speed made it almost impossible to shake him off the ball. Armed with a magical left foot, his free kicks were a joy to behold. If that were not enough, his work rate and passing of the ball gave him an outstanding array of skills. Maradona missed the 1978 World Cup finals (when only 17) as coach Cesar Menotti left him out because of his youth, although he had recently helped his country to victory in the World Youth Championships. At club level he scored 116 goals in 166 games for Argentinos Juniors and they soon realised that they would not be able to hold on to his talent for very long. In 1981 he moved on to Boca Juniors where he scored 40 goals in 28 games before they, too, found that they could not afford to keep him. The following year he was sold to Barcelona for what was, at the time, the highest fee ever paid for a footballer: £3 million. As a 21-year-old, it was obvious that Maradona's potential was limitless and it was only a matter of time before he proved it. Going to Spain with high hopes, he instead showed glimpses of his temperament and a tendency to suffer tantrums. In his first season for Barça he scored 22 times in 36 appearances but despite this his spell at the Nou Camp Stadium was not the happiest of his career. The time encompassed his disastrous World Cup debut and he missed most of his second season as a result of a horrendous tackle that caused a serious achilles tendon injury. Two years later he broke the transfer record again when he was sold to Italian club Napoli for £5

Mexico 1986. Diego Maradona cuts through the Belgium defence during their World Cup Semi-final clash.

million. He fared much better in Serie A helping the club to a domestic league and cup double in 1986-87, victory in the UEFA Cup (1989) and a second league title in 1990.

In the first game of the 1982 World Cup finals against Belgium, Argentina played virtually their 1978 World Cup winning side, adding the talents of Maradona and Ramon Diaz to the stars that had lifted the trophy in Argentina. Maradona made his debut on his home ground in

Barcelona and although he was the victim of several cynical tackles the team produced an outstanding performance. Mario Kempes, the hero of 1978, had few chances to repeat his success and did little. As the South Americans pushed forward in search of victory, the ball broke to the Belgians and Vandenbergh fired in a left-foot shot from the edge of the penalty area to give his team an undeserved win. In their second group game against Hungary, Argentina found the net on no less than four occasions

Spain 1982. Maradona (left) leaves Claudio Gentile of Italy in his wake during this Group C encounter.

with the East Europeans replying only once. Bertoni opened the scoring in the 26th minute and almost immediately afterwards Maradona scored his first World Cup goal, pouncing on a rebound and forcing the ball into the net. Ten minutes after half time, Maradona scored his second before Ossie Ardiles got their fourth. Poloskei pulled one back 14 minutes from time for Hungary. Maradona had arrived on the world

stuck to him as close as his shirt did. The second half saw the Italians take the South Americans by surprise. They came out playing attacking football and Argentina, still suffering from their first half bruises, were taken unawares as Marco Tardelli finished off a counter attack to make it 1-0. Maradona hit a post from a free kick but it was Italy's Cabrini who scored the second goal in the 68th minute. Passarella pulled one back from a

Spain 1982. Diego Maradona covers his face in panic during his clash with the formidable Italian's.

scene, even though the Argentinians were far from their best. They moved into the second phase with a dismal victory over the minnows of El Salvador when they looked nothing more than an average team. In the second round they were drawn to meet one of the favourites, Italy, again in Barcelona. A crowd of 43,000 turned out to watch these two supposedly great teams in action. The game began and finished as a highly physical encounter. The first half was a dour 45 minutes as Italy stifled the opposition with Claudio Gentile literally marking Maradona every time he could. Maradona soon knew how the great Pelé must have felt in 1966 as Gentile

free kick, but the defeat left Argentina needing to defeat Brazil in the second group game. This Brazilian team was the best since their great World Cup winning side of 1970. Boasting players of the calibre of Zico, Falcao and Socrates, they took Argentina apart with sweet, skilful one touch moves that left the watching 44,000 crowd gasping. Zico put the Brazilians ahead in only the 12th minute after Eder's dipping and swerving free kick beat keeper Fillol before crashed down off the underside of the bar. Zico, ever alert, just beat colleague Serginho to the ball and tapped it over the line for 1-0. Maradona was just a poor spectator along with

Mexico 1986. The greatest player in the world thinks nothing of taking on the world. Maradona meets Belgium in the semi-final.

the rest of his team-mates as the Argentinians could do little to stop, never mind match, the samba-driven Brazilian maestros. It was not until the 67th minute that Serginho added a second and then defender Junior danced to the samba beat after finishing off a masterful five-man move on 72 minutes. Maradona's frustration grew and he was eventually sent off shortly before the end for a nasty kick on an opponent. Diaz pulled a solitary strike back for Argentina, but the 3-1 defeat ended Argentina's hopes of retaining the trophy. The team in general and Maradona in particular had failed miserably.

Four years later in Mexico, Argentina were back. Now favourites to win the competition, they steamrollered over their opposition. Maradona was the king of football and rightly so. In their first match in Group A they faced minnows South Korea. Although he failed to score, he had

Mexico 1986. 'The Hand Of God'. Diego Maradona punches the ball past England's Peter Shilton and into the net during their Quarter-final clash at the Azteca Stadium, Mexico City. Amazingly the goal was allowed to stand and Argentina won 2-1.

a hand in all three of his country's goals. The first came after only five minutes. After being brought down, Maradona saw his free kick rebound from the defensive wall back to him before he played the ball to waiting striker Valdano. Valdano's angled shot flashed by the Korean goalkeeper Yun-Kyo and into the net. The second came in similar fashion after 17 minutes. The Koreans conceded another free kick and the little Argentinian floated the ball over the wall for the waiting Ruggeri to head the ball home. In the first minute of the second half he sent over a teasing cross that left the Korean defence in disarray. Valdano tapped in for number three. The Koreans pulled a goal back in the 75th minute but that was it and the match finished at 3-1. Three days later Argentina faced the might of Italy in Puebla. This was the fourth time these teams had met in the finals, but the South Americans had yet to record a win. Italy had won the tournament no less than three times and Argentina once. Maradona and company were favourites to win this clash of titans but went a goal behind after only five minutes when the referee awarded a penalty after the ball struck the unlucky Garre on the arm. Despite the protests of the Argentinian players, Altobelli stepped up and scored from the spot kick, sending 'keeper Pumpido the wrong way. Just before half time, the magical Maradona

outstripped his marker and stroked the ball home brilliantly from an acute angle for the equaliser. Italy might have secured victory in the closing stages when Conti shot against the post, but both teams faded and settled for the draw. A 2-0 win over Bulgaria with goals from Valdano and Burruchaga took Argentina through to the next round. They approached the second phase with more confidence than in 1982, indeed they had good reason to – they had the world's best player in their team. To get through to the quarter-finals they needed to dispose of the team that beat them in the very first World Cup final 56 years earlier – Uruguay. Valdano had a chance to open the scoring but squandered it. Maradona then hit the crossbar with a 30-yard free kick. Pasculli scored the only goal of the game in the 41st minute. A thunderstorm prevented the teams making a game of it in the second half, though the little man was in sparkling form. Argentina were through to the quarter-finals. Two days later, Bobby Robson's rejuvenated England beat Paraguay to set up what would be the confrontation of the tournament. Maradona's quarter-final goals against an unlucky England side will be remembered for both good and bad reasons. The first, in the 56th minute, was clearly handball – jumping for a loose ball with Peter Shilton, he appeared to rise above the England 'keeper

Mexico 1986. Maradona's infamous 'goal'.

(who was five inches taller) and head home. Shilton and the England players immediately surrounded the referee, who, along with his two linesmen must have been the only people present who had not seen the Argentinian's hand flick the ball on. The remainder of the second half saw England pressing for the equaliser only to fall victim to a truly brilliant goal. Spinning away from two midfield players, still within his own half of the pitch, Maradona ran down the inside right channel of the pitch, ever onward in his assault on Shilton's goal. He then outpaced Peter Reid, cut inside central defender Terry Fenwick and as the 'keeper approached he feinted leaving the England man on his backside. Terry Butcher dived in for a final last gasp effort but the ball slid into the net for one of the greatest goals in the history of the tournament. England pulled one back through a Gary Lineker header in the 81st minute, but it was insufficient and the South Americans went through. Maradona famously said after the match that his goal was from 'La Manos De Dios' (The

Hand of God). Three days later, the Argentinians and the owner of 'The Hand of God' walked on to the pitch in the Aztec Stadium in Mexico City to face Belgium in the semi-finals. Maradona was on the top of his form, scoring another two breathtaking goals. In the 51st minute, Enrique delivered a pass into what seemed like an empty space just inside the Belgian penalty area. Maradona accelerated into the gap leaving two defenders for dead, collected the ball and the outside of his left foot did the rest. Goalkeeper Pfaff had no chance. A second goal 12 minutes later killed the game. This time the little Argentinian surged past three defenders into the penalty area before clipping a sweet shot into the corner of the net. The final was set. Europe against South America, West Germany having beaten an unlucky France for the second time in successive World Cup semi-finals. Would the German forward Karl Heinz Rummenigge collect a winners' medal or would Diego Maradona finally stamp his talent in the biggest game of his life? Rummenigge was clearly not fit but played anyway. Lothar Matthäus was given the job of marking Maradona. With hindsight, this was a mistake by the German coach Franz Beckenbauer. Indeed, had Beckenbauer himself not complained when his obvious talents were wasted in marking England's Bobby Charlton back in the summer of 1966? The first Argentinian goal came after Maradona had been fouled by Matthäus, who collected a booking for his efforts. Jorge Burrachaga sent in a high free kick that evaded German goalkeeper Schumacher and Brown headed into an unguarded net. The Germans came back strongly but could not equalise. Shortly after half time it was 2-0. Hector Enrique sent Jorge Valdano through to beat Schumacher. The Germans looked out of it until, in the 75th minute, Rummenigge pulled one back from a corner by Andreas Brehme. This gave them fresh spirit and they equalised through substitute Rudi Voller, only for Burruchaga to score the winner after he had been set up with a glorious pass from Maradona. Although the little man had failed to score in the final he lifted the World Cup trophy as team captain. It was his tournament and if one man ever made a team, it was Diego Maradona.

Italia '90 was to be Maradona's last World Cup, or so it was believed. Yet another disappointing Argentinian side were beaten 1-0 in the opening game against lowly Cameroon, this after the Africans were reduced to nine men after having two players dismissed. Maradona, playing from midfield, was overweight and out of form, failing to impress his home fans. By now, the Italian love affair he had enjoyed had gone sour. Argentina, though playing in his home stadium in Naples, were booed by the fans. They made three changes for the next game against the Soviet Union, starting with Claudio Caniggia who had done well as a substitute against the Cameroon. The Soviets had lost their opening game against Romania and the fact that both teams needed a win set up a remarkable encounter so early in the tournament. Ten minutes into the game, the

Mexico 1986. Maradona (top) flies through the air after a challenge by West German goalkeeper Harald Schumacher.

South Americans lost their goalkeeper Pumpido with a double fracture of the leg. After desperately trying to clear the ball, he had collided with a colleague. Substitute 'keeper Sergio Goycochea came on in his place. Several minutes later, 'The Hand of God' struck again. Following a corner, a certain goal was averted when Maradona, back helping his defence and standing almost on the goal line stopped the ball going into the net by the use of his forearm. It was deliberate handball but the referee, Swedish official Erik Fredriksson waived play on. FIFA later

ensure passage to the second phase. Maradona, again out of sorts, delivered a fine corner kick for defender Monzon to head home the first goal in the 60th minute. Balint equalised five minutes later. In phase two, Argentina again faced their great rivals, the boys from Brazil. Brazil were the form team of the two, having won all their first round games with flair and skill, and were clear favourites to win through to the quarter-finals. After dominating the match, subduing the less than fit Maradona and hitting the post twice, Brazil fell victims to a flash of the little man's

Italy 1990. Referee Edgardo Codesal Mendez (centre) explains the coin toss to the two captains, Argentina's Diego Maradona (left) and West Germany's Lothär Matthaüs before the World Cup Final. Germany winning 1-0 in a disappointing match.

criticised the official's judgment and sent him home early. That decision, however, did not help the Soviet team and minutes later Argentina went ahead through Troglio after Maradona had sent over a corner. Although the Soviets had a man dismissed for pulling at Caniggia's shirt, they subdued the world champions and looked ever increasingly like they would at least equalise. In the 79th minute, however, Argentina added their second and killer goal. Burruchaga, out of form and playing on his reputation like so many of his team-mates, intercepted a back pass to score easily. In the final game, both Argentina and their opponents Romania needed only a point to

genius. In the 80th minute he broke away from three opponents in the centre of the field and slipped the ball to the hard running Caniggia, who rounded 'keeper Taffarel before stroking a left-foot shot into the net. Brazil collapsed. Captain Ricardo Gomes was sent off for fouling Basualdo. In the dying minutes, Muller had a glorious opportunity to equalise, but the talented winger shot wide. Argentina had at last beaten their rivals in the finals for the first time even though it had been achieved against the run of play. The quarter-final encounter between Argentina and Yugoslavia was a 0-0 game that hardly produced any excitement in the 120

Mexico 1986. Diego Maradona lifts the World Cup, Argentina are World Champions for the second time.

minutes of play. Despite being down to ten men for all but 30 minutes of the game, the Slavs were the more impressive of the two sides. The tie went to penalty kicks, the South Americans winning 3-2, although the crowd showed their delight as Maradona, yet to score in the competition, missed his chance and tamely tapped his kick at goalkeeper Ivkovic. In the semi-final, held in the Stadio San Paolo in Naples, Italian revelation Salvatori Schillaci opened the scoring netting his fifth goal of the tournament on 17 minutes. Caniggia equalised in the 67th minute but the match went to extra time. The Argentinians then lost defender Giusti, dismissed for an off-the-ball incident with Roberto Baggio, but with no further goals penalties were required once more. The first three players from each side successfully converted their efforts. Goalkeeper Goycochea then saved Donadoni's spot kick and Maradona strode up and scored his. Goycochea saved Serena's effort and Argentina were in their second successive World Cup final although they hardly deserved it. West Germany defeated a gallant England side in a similar penalty shoot-out in the other semi-final and so the final teams were the same as in 1986. West Germany avenged their earlier defeat with an Andy Brehme penalty nine minutes from time after Rudi Voller had been fouled in the box. Argentina, missing the banned Caniggia, were clearly playing for penalties. They became the first country in World Cup history to have a player sent off in the final late in the second half, and a second followed before the final whistle.

Maradona himself was lucky not to have been sent for an early bath as he was booked for jostling the referee.

Undoubtedly the greatest player in the world at the time of the 1986 competition, Diego Maradona was an average player just four years later. At the end of the 1990-91 season he had tested positive for cocaine and was banned from the game for 15 months, first in Italy and then the world. Naples turned its back on him and he returned to Argentina a somewhat pathetic broken man, overweight and troubled at the age of 31. He was arrested in a further drug-related incident shortly after his return and ordered by the judge to quit his addiction or face a jail sentence. His ban completed, Napoli wanted him to return to Italy. He refused and instead signed for Seville in Spain in 1992. Another disastrous year followed and he moved back to Argentina, signing this time for Newell's Old Boys but he was soon sacked for missing training. In 1994, the World Cup shifted continents again and the finals were played in the United States. Maradona, evidently forgiven by the Argentinian authorities returned to the squad, slimmer, fitter and in peak form. After scoring a stunning goal against Greece, which turned out to be the last for his country, he was selected for a random drug test. To the surprise of everyone, he tested positive for the banned substance ephedrine and as a result he was sent home and banned from the game once more. At 33, his international career was over and his shining example of how to play the beautiful game was overshadowed by his behaviour off the field. He fired an air rifle upon news reporters camped outside his villa in Buenos Aires and was fined by the local authorities. He pleaded that the newsmen were upsetting his family and that they should leave him alone. He later made a come back with Boca Juniors, but again failed a drugs test after only his second game. In 1999 a desperate Maradona found help for his addictions in Cuba, where he befriended Premier Fidel Castro. He was diagnosed with a heart condition brought on by drug and alcohol abuse. Now in his forties, Maradona is a shadow of the footballing genius who was once the greatest player in the world.

Mexico 1986. Diego strutting his stuff against South Korea.

LINEKER
MR NICE GUY

GARY LINEKER

ENGLAND

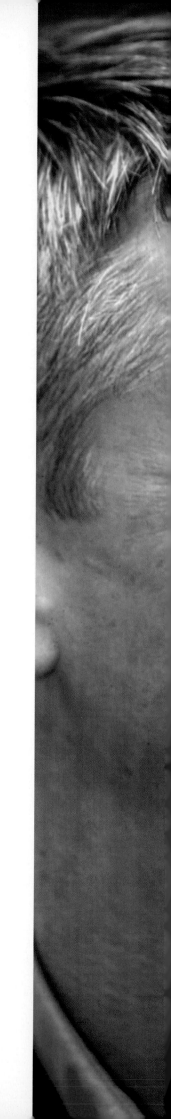

G ary Lineker was a striker with tremendous speed and finishing ability and the uncanny knack of being in the right place at the right time to score his goals. He also had a reputation for fair play and despite being on the receiving end of some rough treatment over his career he was never booked or sent off. Gary Winston Lineker was born in Leicester on 30 November 1960 and began his career at 17 playing with his local club Leicester City. He made his senior debut against Oldham Athletic on New Year's Day 1979, but it was not until the 1981-82 campaign that he won a regular place in the starting line-up. After initially playing in a wide role he switched to become an out-and-out striker and began to score regularly, finishing as City's leading scorer each season between 1981-82 and 1984-85. He won his first cap for England against Scotland in May 1984 before moving on to join Everton for a fee of £800,000 in the summer of 1985. Although he stayed for just one season he made his mark, scoring 40 goals for the Merseysiders. That season was his first taste of the big time as the Toffees narrowly missed out to city rivals Liverpool, finishing as runners-up in the League and losing by a 3-1 margin in the FA Cup final when Lineker netted his side's only goal. His efforts earned him the title of 'Footballer of the Year' from both the PFA and the Football Writers' Association and after performing well in the 1986 World Cup finals he was sold to Spanish giants Barcelona, then managed by Terry Venables, for £2.5 million. He stayed in Spain for three years, helping Barça win both the Copa del Rey (1988) and the European Cup Winners' Cup (1989). By this time Venables had left the Nou Camp for Tottenham and in July 1989 he brought the striker back to England. Lineker made another appearance in the FA Cup final of 1991 when Spurs met Brian Clough's Nottingham Forest. This time, Gary picked up a winners' medal as the North London club won the match 2-1, though he became only the second man to miss a penalty in an FA Cup final.

Gary Lineker scored 48 goals in 80 appearances for England after an uneasy start to his international career. He made his debut against Scotland at Hampden Park in May 1984, coming on from the substitutes' bench. The game ended in a 1-1 draw, Tony Woodcock scoring England's goal. In the summer of 1986, England flew to Mexico having qualified by winning their group, the squad having high hopes of a glorious

Mexico 1986. Gary Lineker spins around in delight after scoring against Poland in the second round. England went on to win the game 3-0 with Lineker netting a hat-trick.

campaign. Then, just before the tournament began Lineker thought he had broken his arm in training but, fortunately for him and England, the injury turned out to be a bad strain. After consulting the team doctor, manager Bobby Robson included him in the line-up as his main

Mexico 1986. Gary celebrates his hat-trick following the Poland game. He went on to win the Golden Boot as the tournaments leading scorer with six goals.

striker. In the first game, England played the team who they had beaten to reach the World Cup final in 1966, Portugal. Then, Portugal were a formidable side, boasting the talents of the great Eusebio and the tall, gangly winger, Torres. Eusebio was long gone by now, and Torres was now team coach, albeit of a very poor side. Surely England could not lose. Early in the game Lineker, who had missed training because of the arm injury and was clearly not 100 per cent fit, missed two chances to put his team ahead. As the game went on Portugal, by now swamping the midfield, clearly became the dominant team although they seemed to pose little attacking threat. A draw looked odds on, despite the fact that England's midfield seemed unable to command the ball, even when they managed to retrieve it from the Portuguese. Then Portugal broke away and scored the only goal of the game following bad defensive errors. England were stunned and couldn't have made a worse

start to the competition. Manager Bobby Robson came under attack immediately from a very hostile English press. The next group game, against Morocco, was almost as disastrous. England stumbled their way to a 0-0 draw and their World Cup looked at an end. A bad shoulder injury put captain Bryan Robson out of the tournament and AC Milan midfielder Ray Wilkins was out for two games after he threw the ball at the referee and was sent off. Wilkins has the unenviable record of having been the first England player to be sent off in the finals. England improved in the second half but could not break down the Africans. The fans jeered the team as they left the stadium. England were in deep trouble. Necessity rather than choice meant that there were several changes to the line-up for the final group game against old rivals Poland. In came Peter Reid and Steve Hodge for Robson and Wilkins while Trevor Steven and Peter Beardsley replaced Chris Waddle and Mark

Italy 1990. Lineker scoring England's equaliser against West Germany in the Semi-final. The match finished 1-1 with England going out 4-3 on penalties.

Italy 1990. England World Cup Team. Back row (left to right) Peter Beardsley, Terry Butcher, Gary Lineker, Alvin Martin, Gary Stevens, Peter Shilton. Front row (left to right) Trevor Steven, Peter Reid, Steve Hodge, Glenn Hoddle, Kenny Sansom.

Hateley. Lineker himself faced the axe but instead turned up with a hat-trick to send England through to the next round. He has since described his first goal in that game as the goal that 'changed my life'. In the next phase, Lineker scored two against Paraguay, England winning 3-0 despite some desperate and crude tackling by the South American defenders and one against Argentina in the quarter-final as Maradona's 'Hand of God' goal led to their defeat and exit from the competition. Nevertheless, Lineker was leading scorer in the Mexico World Cup tournament with 6 goals.

Now established as one of the fastest and deadliest strikers in the world, one of Gary Lineker's many high spots for England came in Madrid in February 1987. England were playing a strong Spanish side and a draw would have been a good result. However, facing his club 'keeper and friend Zubizarreta, he put four goals past a bewildered Spanish defence as England romped home 4-2. In the 1988 European Championships in Germany, England were amongst the favourites to win the competition. They failed miserably and lost all three of their opening group matches. In the first game against the Republic of Ireland, Lineker missed at least six gilt-edged chances before the Irish scored the winning goal. In the second game against Holland he hit the post. England conceded seven goals

and scored only twice through Bryan Robson against Holland and Tony Adams against the Soviet Union. Lineker was substituted in the second and third games and was later diagnosed as suffering from hepatitis. Two years later in the Italia '90 World Cup, he scored four more goals as England reached the semi-finals and thus joined the ranks of the elite goal-scorers who have netted a total of ten times in the World Cup finals. Had the penalty shoot-out system in the semi-final against eventual winners West Germany counted, he would have equalled Bobby Charlton's 22-year record of 49 goals. Disappointingly, it was not to be. Lineker was on course to beat the record, but after his baby son was diagnosed as having leukaemia in 1991 he obviously had other things on his mind. He failed to hit the target in his last six internationals, his leanest spell for England. He missed a penalty in his final appearance at Wembley in the 1-1 draw with Brazil in 1992. England went to Sweden for the European Championships feeling confident that they would reach the semi-final if not the final itself, but they failed miserably, as they had in Germany four years before. With Bobby Robson gone, Graham Taylor, the new England manager, seemed intent on playing Lineker in a wide role most of the time. The team's performances against Yugoslavia and France were well below par and both games ended 0-0, although full back Stuart Pearce was most unlucky when he

Mexico 1986. Lineker gives the Poland defence the run-around.

struck the French crossbar from a tremendous free kick. The final group game against Sweden turned out to be Lineker's last game for England. Graham Taylor (who had considered dropping Lineker from his squad when he took over as manager in 1990 but changed his mind and instead made him captain) substituted him before the end of the game. England were 2-1 down with only minutes to go, and as he came off the pitch the player was clearly disappointed

Italy 1990. Lineker scores from the penalty spot against Cameroon to help England on their way to a 3-2 win.

Lineker is substituted in the 1992 European Championship game against Sweden at Råsundastadion, Solna. Graham Taylor secured his place in the fans' bad books by taking off his captain. Lineker was never capped again, a downbeat end to a sparkling career.

at being replaced. Gary Lineker scored four hat-tricks for England, two of them against Turkey. After the European Championships of 1992, he announced he was to leave England for the newly formed professional league in Japan. He signed for Nagoya Grampus Eight but only scored one goal following the reoccurrence of a toe injury. He now enjoys heading the BBC's football coverage team and the Walkers brand of crisps carry not only his face on their advertising, but also his name.

PLATINI
TRÉS BON

MICHEL PLATINI

FRANCE

Michel François Platini was born in Joeuf on 21 June 1955, the grandson of Italian immigrants, and went on to become France's greatest player. His early career was spent with his local club – AS Jouef – and shortly before his 17th birthday he signed for AS Nancy-Lorraine where his father was on the coaching staff. A regular in the first team by by the age of 17, he was drafted into the French army for his national service when he reached 19. Naturally, he captained the army football team. Out of the service, Platini marked his full international debut by scoring a goal in a 2-2 draw against Czechoslovakia at the age of 20 in March 1976. Platini also represented France in the Olympic Games that same year and the team reached the quarter-finals before falling to East Germany. Two years later he gained his first honour at club level, scoring the winner for Nancy in their victory over Nice to take the French Cup.

Platini then gave the world a glimpse of his potential, proving to be one of the top players in the 1978 World Cup finals in Argentina. He played in the centre of midfield, leading an improved French squad that would later dominate Europe throughout the early eighties. A year after that World Cup campaign, he moved to AS Saint-Etienne having scored 98 goals in seven years for Nancy. He tasted defeat in the 1981 and 1982 French Cup finals but added almost 60 goals to his account for AS Saint-Etienne in his three seasons there. He collected a French championship medal in 1981 and was a championship runner-up in 1982. Italian giants Inter Milan became increasingly interested in signing the Frenchman but inexplicably let him slip through their grasp and he was sold to Juventus in 1982 for a fee of £1.2m. His drive and goals helped Juve win the Serie A title three times in five years as well as being runner-up twice in that period. The Frenchman scored no less than 36 goals in his first two seasons in Italy. In 1984 he was in the Juventus side that defeated FC Porto 2-1 to win the European Cup Winners' Cup. Later that summer he scored in every round as France went on to win the European Championship on their home soil. His tally of nine made him the tournament's leading scorer and included hat-tricks in the victories over Belgium and Yugoslavia. Michel Platini went on to score a total of 41 goals for his country, well in excess of

European Cup Winners Cup 1984. Juventus' Michel Platini (l) tackles Manchester United's Paul McGrath (r)

World Cup legend Just Fontaine and still a record for the national team. He was also voted 'European Footballer of the Year' in three consecutive years (1983 to 1985). In 1985 he lifted the European Cup for Juventus after converting the winning penalty in the tragic game at Heysel against Liverpool.

For the 11th World Cup series, hosted by Argentina in 1978, manager Michel Hidalgo played what was to become the backbone of that great French team of the 1980s. Platini and Maxime Bossis dominated the midfield, the giant Marius Trésor in defence and the pacy and skilful winger Didier Six all played in the first group

European Championship 1984. Belgium goalkeeper Jean Marie Pfaff appeals for offside as France's Michel Platini (far left) turns away to celebrate the goal.

game against Italy. France enjoyed the most perfect start as Bernard Lacombe rammed the ball past the startled Italian goalkeeper Dino Zoff after just 31 seconds. Italy rough and tumbled through the game, Paulo Rossi equalised in the 29th minute before substitute Renato Zaccarelli scored what turned out to be the winner shortly after the break. France lost their second group game against eventual winners and hosts Argentina despite outplaying their opponents for most of the first period, Platini dominating the midfield. Six was blatantly fouled in the penalty area but the referee overruled French appeals for a spot kick. Then, Argentina's central defender and skipper Daniel Passarella himself scored from a disputed penalty kick in the very last seconds of the first half. Centre half Marius Trésor, who was having an outstanding game, tackled Mario Kempes brilliantly but then fell over his own feet.

sweep in the rebound. The French were level, which was less than they deserved. Platini almost scored late in the game as did Didier Six but the South Americans kept them at bay and found a winner 18 minutes from time through the moustachioed Leopoldo Luque. France were now eliminated from the tournament. In their final group game they met Hungary and ran out 3-1 winners but it was too late. The match was one of the most exciting of the competition, all four goals came in the first half and three of them in a glorious five-minute spell. Lopez scored first for the French before Berdoll ran through four tackles to hit a great individual goal. Hungary pulled one back through Zombori but Rocheteau netted straight from the restart. France finished a disappointing third in their group. They deserved much more.

Spain 1982. Platini of France (r) shoots for goal against Czechoslovakia in the Group Four match.

The referee, only yards from the scene, controversially awarded the home team a penalty. In the 60th minute, justice was restored when the enigmatic Dominique Rocheteau shot against the crossbar and Platini was there to

Four years later France came through their qualifying round in second place on goal difference behind Belgium, thus eliminating a struggling Dutch side long past their wonderful 'total football' era. In the finals they were drawn

European Cup 1985. Juventus' Michel Platini scores the winning goal from a penalty kick against Liverpool in the final.

in a group along with England, Czechoslovakia and Kuwait. The first game against England was played in a temperature of 100 degrees Fahrenheit and the French fell behind to the fastest goal ever scored in the history of the World Cup, Bryan Robson volleying home from a throw in on the right after just 27 seconds. France never fully recovered despite equalising

Mexico 1986. Platini in deep concentration before the Group C game against Hungary.

through Gérard Soler in the 25th minute. Half time arrived with the teams level. On 66 minutes Robson again scored, this time with a glorious flying header. England completed the scoring eight minutes from time when Ipswich centre forward Paul Mariner netted from close range. For Platini and the rest of his team, it looked like Argentina all over again. Minnows Kuwait were now waiting for France. Genghini scored from a free kick after 30 minutes to give France the lead and Platini added another on 42 minutes with a shot from the edge of the penalty box. Didier Six hit the third just after the half-time break, volleying past 'keeper Al Tarabulsi. Kuwait scored a consolation goal through Al Buloushi before Bossis scored the fourth goal of the game in the last minute. In their final group game against Czechoslovakia, France only needed a draw to go into the second round while their opponents required a win to proceed. The French defence played their best game of the tournament frustrating the Czechs on numerous occasions, although both sides had opportunities to take the lead. After a goalless first half, with France rocking slightly, Didier Six put his side ahead when he scored from close range. Czechoslovakia equalised with a penalty by Panenka after 84 minutes and in the closing stages the Czech striker Vizek was sent off for apparently kicking Platini. France, at last, were through to the second phase after finishing as runners-up in their group behind England. Faced with an apparently 'easy' group they made a meal of the first game against Austria winning by a single goal, scored by Genghini from a free kick. Winger Dominique Rocheteau tormented the Austrian defence after coming on as a 11th minute substitute for the injured Bernard

Mexico 1986. French Captain Michel Platini celebrates a goal during the World Cup quarter-final against Brazil at the Jalisco Stadium in Guadalajara, Mexico.

Lacombe. Rocheteau, on a typical run, was brought down six minutes from half time. With Platini out of the game through injury, up stepped Genghini who struck his kick into the Austrian net via an upright. The game against Northern Ireland proved to be one of France's finest hours. Two goals apiece from Alain Giresse and Dominique Rocheteau demonstrated the difference in class between the two teams. Gerry Armstrong scored a consolation goal for the Irish when France were coasting at 3-0. They were now in the last four and looking stronger with every game.

By far the most exciting game of the 1982 tournament was the semi-final clash between France and West Germany. This game had everything that is good about the game featured in it – and everything that is bad. The enthralling encounter was played before 63,000 people in the Sanchez Stadium, Seville and the eyes of millions of people sat in their homes watching on television. France, with the exception of the Brazilians, were the most attractive team in the competition and their captain was at his positive best, testing the German defence and midfield with his superb passing. Their weak link was their goalkeeper Jean-Luc Ettori. In the 18th minute,

the unfortunate 'keeper failed to hold on to a shot by Pierre Littbarski. Germany were ahead. Platini rallied his men well and nine minutes later Dominique Rocheteau was pulled down in the penalty area by German defender Bernd Forster. Platini claimed the ball, kissing it as he placed it on the penalty spot, before smashing it past goalkeeper Shumacher to level the scores. The game was at stalemate when, midway through the second half, French substitute Battiston ran onto a through ball from Platini. Everybody watching was convinced the Frenchman would score – even the Schumacher – but as Battiston played the ball past him the German 'keeper smashed into him in a very deliberate effort to stop him. The ball missed the goal and went out of play. Battiston lay unconscious for several minutes, as the French quite rightly demanded a penalty. Schumacher should have been sent off for one of the most blatant fouls ever seen in the World Cup. Instead, Battiston was carried off the field on a stretcher. The French got nothing for the incident and the 'keeper was not even spoken to by the referee. Both sides had chances to win the game either side of the Battiston incident but failed to do so. Normal time came and went and the teams moved into extra-time. Two minutes into the first period, central

European Championship 1984. A cockerel, the national symbol of France, strolls down the sideline past France's Michel Platini during the Group One match against Yugoslavia.

defender Marius Trésor, in the German penalty box after the French had been awarded a free kick, volleyed home a spectacular goal. Six minutes later, Giresse helped himself to a goal with another spectacular shot from the edge of the West German penalty area. France led 3-1 with only 12 minutes to go. Surely, they were in their first final? The German manager Jupp Derwall sent a half-fit Karl-Heinz Rummenigge into the fray as a do-or-die act two minutes before France's third goal. The substitution worked. The striker had been on the pitch barely six minutes before pulling the score back to 3-2, flicking the ball past Ettori from a low Littbarski cross. This goal lifted the Germans. Tired legs were suddenly rejuvenated while French heads were going down. Two minutes into the second period, veteran Horst Hrubesch headed a centre back into the French penalty for Klaus Fischer to score with a spectacular overhead kick. 3-3. French confidence dropped lower. The game ended and a new rule came into operation – a cruel penalty shoot-out that would decide the finalists for the first time. France took the first kick and Alain Giresse scored. German fullback Kalz equalised. Amoros scored. Breitner equalised. Rocheteau put France ahead 3-2 and then centre half Stielike missed his spot kick. All France need to do was keep their heads-and they were in the World Cup final. Didier Six

stepped forward and missed. The teams were level again. Platini and Rummenigge then scored their kicks and the competition moved into sudden death. Bossis stepped up and Schumacher made a good save. All Hrubesch had to do was keep calm and Germany were in the final. Hrubesch showed his steel-like nerves by arrogantly asking the referee to place the ball on the penalty spot for him. He then sent Ettori the wrong way and Germany, not France, were in the final. The devastated French team left the pitch to learn that their team-mate Battiston had suffered several broken vertebrae and lay seriously injured in a Spanish hospital.

The 1986 World Cup finals were held in Mexico after first choice hosts Colombia had pulled out. Two goals from Platini in France's last qualifying game against Yugoslavia put them into their third tournament in succession. Brazil and Argentina were again the favourites boasting the talents of Zico and Maradona, who was by now arguably the world's greatest player. France faced Canada, Hungary and the Soviet Union in their first round group. The European champions played World Cup debutants Canada in their opening game. The French could be excused for thinking that their opponents would be a push over, but despite the fact that they had most of the play they had to wait a long time for a goal.

Jean-Pierre Papin provided it in the 78th minute and his strike turned out to be the only goal of the game. After having scraped through against the totally unfancied Canadians they now faced a much tougher task against a determined and well-organised Soviet side in their next fixture. Platini struck the post with a 30-yard shot but the first half remained goalless, despite some thrilling football from both sides. The Soviets went ahead in the 53rd minute when striker Rats rasped in a stinger from 30yards. French goalkeeper Bats had no chance and groped thin air as the ball screamed into his net for one of the strikes of the tournament. Luis Fernandez scored the equaliser in the 61st minute, stabbing home after good work from Tigana. With the 1-1 draw, the Soviet Union topped the Group C table with France second only on goal difference. The last group game saw France needing a draw against Hungary to be certain of going through to the second round. For Hungary, nothing less than a win would be sufficient. The East Europeans put a lot of early pressure on the French defence but could not score the goal they needed. Platini was again in masterful form, driving his team-mates ever onward. In the 41st minute, Stopyra scored for France with a header from six yards. Hungary went close early in the second half when midfielder Detari hit the crossbar with a snap shot. The French held out. Then, in the 62nd minute, Rocheteau played a superb ball for Tigana to run on to and make the score 2-0. In the 84th minute, a beautiful cross-goal pass by Platini let in Rocheteau to add a third. France were now one of the favourites win the competition despite finishing the group in second place below the Soviets on goal difference. Their next game was held in the Estadio Olympico '68, Mexico City on 17 June when they faced the holders Italy, who were without the injured Paulo Rossi. The French, however, were at the peak of their powers, with Platini their key man. He scored his first goal of the tournament on 14 minutes after Fernandez fed Rocheteau who in turn passed to Platini, who chipped the ball neatly over the advancing

Platini in joyous mood after Juventus clinched victory over Liverpool in the European Cup Final at the Heysel Stadium in Brussels. Juventus won the match 1-0 although their victory was marred by serious crowd riots.

European Championship 1984. Platini in the Semi Final game, France v Portugal.

Galli's lunge. Fernandez then slammed a 30-yarder against the bar as the French dominated the match. After 57 minutes, France got their second goal through Stopyra from a move that began deep in their own half. Rocheteau laid the ball to Stopyra who tucked it away from the narrowest of angles. France looked like and played like heirs to the throne … would they be finally crowned? In the quarter-finals, they met the past kings of football, the mighty Brazil. France had the upper hand in the opening minutes, seemingly not showing the slightest awe of their opponents. However, despite their flowing football, it was the South Americans who took the lead in the 18th minute through Careca, following a sweet move between Junior and Muller. After half an hour of attacking football from both teams, Muller almost increased Brazil's lead when he fired against the post. In the 41st minute France drew level. Giresse fed Rocheteau whose pass was tapped

home by Platini. The game was now a stalemate and the Brazilian fans began to chant the name of their hero Zico, sat on the substitutes' bench injured. The Brazilian coach bowed to their opinion and sent him on for the last 15 minutes. He had barely entered the fray when Brazil were awarded a penalty following a foul by French 'keeper Bats on full back Branco. The fans chanted for Zico again and the master picked up the ball and placed it on the penalty spot, but he then turned from hero to villain as Bats denied him with a tremendous save. The incident lifted the French, but they could not capitalise on their good fortune and the game ended 1-1. No further goals were added in extra-time, though both goalmouths saw plenty of action, the best chance falling to Bellone four minutes from time. He was fouled on the edge of the penalty area but the referee played the advantage but the player was unable to regain his feet after stumbling from the challenge. The chance was lost through deliberate foul play and the French received nothing for it, their minds must have gone back four years when the referee blew for the end of extra-time and a penalty shoot-out was about to resolve the tie. Socrates missed the first kick for Brazil and Stopyra put his into the net to give the French an early lead. Brazil equalised and Bellone got some consolation when he converted France's third kick. At 3-3, Platini, on his 31st birthday, blasted his spot kick high and wide to increase the pressure on his team-mates. Brazil's Julio Cesar threw away the advantage when he missed his kick. All that Luis Fernandez needed to do now was score and France were in the semi-final once more. Sending Carlos the wrong way, he did not let his team-mates or his country down. The great Brazilians were out, but the French were through and just as four years before they now faced their old adversaries West Germany. Still in the Germany goal was the infamous Harald Schumacher while the man he had seriously injured, Patrick Battiston, was in the French squad. The French seemed to freeze on the day and the midfield, including Platini, was mostly ineffective. Andy Brehme scored from a free kick for the Germans when the ball squeezed under Bats for the opening goal. In the second half Rudi Voller netted the goal that took the game away from the struggling French. Again they had fallen at the semi-final. This World Cup witnessed the end of a truly world class team. A team dedicated to stylish, attacking football, yet lacking that vital ingredient that makes World Cup winners – resilience.

Shortly after the tournament, Platini announced his retirement from football at the age of 31. The football world was stunned. In August 1987, however, the French genius came out of retirement to play for the Rest of the World against the Football League at Wembley, his only appearance there. In total he played 72 full internationals for France, making him fifth in his country's all-time record appearance list behind Deschamps, Amoros, Blanc and Bossis. He was selected as captain on 49 occasions and scored 41 goals. He later took charge of the national side but his team failed to reach the 1990 World Cup finals. They then qualified for the 1992 European Championships in Denmark, but he resigned shortly afterwards following a poor

European Championship 1984. Platini celebrates with his team mates after winning the 1984 Championships against Spain 2-0 at the Parc des Princes, Paris.

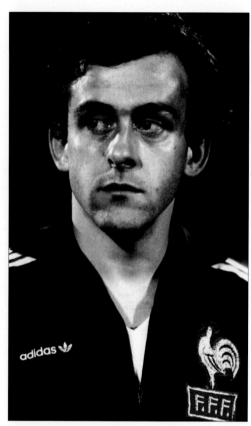

Argentina 1978. Platini before the Group One match against Argentina.

display. Four months later he was installed in the role of co-chairman of the World Cup Organising Committee. in 1994 his lobbying saw FIFA ban the tackle from behind and goalkeepers picking up of the ball from a back pass. In 1998 France at last won the World Cup. Playing on home soil, they beat a demoralised Brazilian side in the final. Alas, the victory came 12 years too late for Platini to take any part on the playing side, although this did not prevent him from standing and applauding from the stands wearing a French national shirt under his suit jacket. Michel Platini can only be described as one the greatest players of his generation, the greatest in French history and one of the best in the world from any era. His career now emulates that of the great Pele, travelling the world as a roving ambassador for football.

MATTHÄUS
THE MACHINE

LOTHAR MATTHÄUS

WEST GERMANY

othar Matthäus was born on 21 March 1961 in Erlangen, West Germany and began his career with FC Herzogenaurach before moving on to Borussia Mönchengladbach, then one of Europe's most successful club sides. He won his first cap against Holland in the 1980 European Championship finals in Italy, but although West Germany won the competition he did not make the final team. In 1984 he was transferred to Bayern München. Bayern were now becoming a force again, winning three consecutive championships and the domestic cup in 1986. He played against Porto in the 1987 European Cup final when the Germans were clear favourites to win the trophy. Bayern took the lead through Kogl who headed past 'keeper Mlynarczyk. Matthäus then played a brilliant through ball to Michael Rummenigge, but the brother of one of West Germany's favourite sons missed the target and screwed his shot wide. Porto came back to win the match late in the game with goals from Madjer and Juary. Matthäus then joined Italian giants Inter Milan in 1988 for a fee of £2.5m, announcing that it was the best career move he'd made to date and that the Italian league was the best in the world. He helped Inter win the Serie A title in 1989 and two years later scored one of their goals in a 2-1 aggregate victory over Roma to secure the UEFA Cup. His surging runs from deep within his own half, coupled with his tremendous shot and endless running made him one the world's finest midfield players.

Lothar Matthäus made his World Cup debut as a substitute against Chile in a 4-1 win on 21 June 1982 in the Spanish town of Oviedo. He was on the bench again in the final group game against Austria when he came on as a second half replacement for the injured Karl-Heinz Rummenigge. Germany won their next game against Austria 1-0, amid a storm of protests, the players of both teams being accused of creating the right result to see them both go through to the next phase. The Germans needed to win to go through, but if they won by a single goal Austria would also go through at the expense of Algeria, who had defeated the Germans in the first game. For the first ten minutes, Germany played well and looked like they were going to bulldoze the Austrians. Then, after 10 minutes Horst Hrubesch headed Germany ahead and both teams seemed to lose all interest merely sitting back and playing the ball around

Italy 1990. West Germany's Lothar Matthäus (L) and Rudi Voller celebrate victory over Argentina in the World Cup Final.

effortlessly for the next 80 minutes. FIFA made no attempt to admonish the countries, but it left a sour taste in the mouth. Matthäus played no further part in the competiton as Germany went on to reach the final where they were defeated by Italy.

By 1986, Matthäus was a regular in the national team. The Mexico World Cup finals brought the Germans up against Uruguay in a group dubbed 'The Group of Death'. They drew their opening match thanks to a late strike from Klaus Allofs. The game was hard and often brutal, the Uruguayans resorting to cynical tactics early on and showing their opponents what kind of game they were in for. In the next game West Germany took on Scotland and beat them 2-1, before losing, surprisingly, 2-1 to Denmark. It did not matter, however, as they had already qualified for the next phase. On 17 June they faced mighty Morocco and duly beat them 1-0 with Matthäus scoring his first World Cup goal three minutes from time. He netted from a 30-yard free kick, having taken his shot before the Moroccans had finished arranging their defensive wall. The Moroccans had frustrated the German attack with their defensive play time and time again, which was more a testament to how badly Germany played rather than how well the Africans performed. Matthäus and his colleagues moved into the quarter-final against the host

nation, Mexico. In the blistering heat of the Azteca Stadium both teams contributed to an ill-tempered match. Eight players were booked and two, Mexico's midfielder Aquirre and Germany's defender Berthold were shown the red card. The normal 90 minutes ended, then another 30 minutes of extra time and neither side had found a breakthrough. It took a penalty shoot-out to produce a winner, Germany running out 4-1 winners with Matthäus, Aloffs, Brehme and Littbarski all scoring from the spot. The West Germans were in the semi-final for a record eighth time - and their opponents were to be Michelle Platini's France. The game was not half the spectacle of the same fixture four years previously. France, who had been drained by their quarter-final victory over Brazil, were hardly in the game. The Germans, sensing their opponents' weariness, played to their strengths and took the lead after only eight minutes through full back Andy Brehme's free kick. The French came alive for a spell in the second half, but could not beat Schumacher in the German goal. Voller scored a breakaway goal in the last seconds to enable the Germans to reach their second consecutive World Cup final and their fifth overall. Their opponents were Argentina who could be tough if need be, but were the flair team on the day. Germany's game was one of determination and they did not have a single player in their squad to match the skill and magic of Maradona. Playing in midfield, Argentinian Jorge Burruchaga dominated, while Matthäus was given a similar job to that of Franz Beckenbauer 20 years previously – to man mark the opposition's key man. In 1966, Beckenbauer had followed Bobby Charlton everywhere, thus denying the team his skills as a playmaker. Lothar Matthäus was to do the same with Maradona, and like Beckenbauer before him, he failed. The assumption was that Argentina were a one-man team, and the theory was simple - stop

the German stop him probing forward, ran around in circles. Even though he marked his man tightly, Maradona's skill with the ball enabled him to dominate his marker. Maradona spun and for a second lost Matthäus, who could only watch as his clinical pass freed Enrique, who passed to Valdano, sprinting through the German defence. Valdano drew Schumacher off his line before coolly slipping the ball past him for the second goal. Then it seems Germany realised their mistake and freed Matthäus form his

European Championship 2000. A tired looking Lothar Matthäus of Germany, winning his 150th cap in the Group A match against Portugal.

Maradona and you stop Argentina. The Germans, to their ultimate cost, got it wrong. The Argentinians went 1-0 up and it was Matthäus who gave away the decisive free kick after a crunching tackle on Maradona. The kick was swung over by Burruchaga leaving goalkeeper Schumacher punching fresh air for a change and the ball met the head of Brown, who powerful despatched it into the German net. The second half continued where the first had ended. Matthäus, still for the most part ineffective against Maradona who seemed content to let

position of destroyer. It proved to be a masterstroke. First Rummenigge pulled one back and then Voller equalised. Sadly for them, the celebrations were over before they had begun for Maradona, free now, delivered a defence-splitting ball through to Burruchaga. The Argentinian showed his class as he, too, drew the goalkeeper before scoring the third, and winning goal. Two consecutive World Cup final defeats weighed heavily on the German team. Could they pull themselves up and create a new team for the finals in Italy, four years away?

USA 1994. Matthäus gets ready for their World Cup opening game against Bolivia.

By the time Italia '90 came around, Matthäus was team captain and the Germans kicked off their campaign in the magnificent San Siro stadium in Milan with an emphatic 4-1 victory against Yugoslavia. Matthäus scored two of the goals himself, one of which was a typical long-range stunner after running powerfully through the opposition midfield. Their next game against the United Arab Emirates produced an emphatic 5-1 victory, Matthäus again scoring, this time with the aid of a deflection. Their third and final group match was a disappointing 1-1 draw with a skilful Colombian side. West Germany finished top of their group and moved on to meet great rivals Holland in the next phase. Unfortunately the match will be remembered for all the wrong reasons. The Dutch goalkeeper van Breukelen conned the referee into sending German striker Rudi Voller off the field for allegedly kicking him. As Voller walked off the pitch, Dutch midfielder

Frank Rijkaard spat at him and also received a red card. The Germans finally overpowered the more skilful Dutch team and came away winners by 2-1, in one of the better games of the competition. Franz Beckenbauer's team moved past a vastly improved Czechoslovakian side in the quarter-finals thanks to a Matthäus penalty in a tight game. In the 25th minute, Klinsmann rounded two defenders before being fouled in the box. Matthäus sent Yugoslavian keeper Stejskal the wrong way with his powerful kick. Germany had several chances to go further ahead either side of half time, but excellent defensive work form the Slavs denied them further goals. Although the Czechs had Moravcik sent off in the 65th minute, they put West Germany through their paces and Matthäus' colleagues knew they had been in a tough game. The machine rumbled on into their ninth semi-final appearance. Next, England. West Germany were the team of the tournament so far and started favourites to beat their old adversaries at the Stadio Delle Alpi, Turin on the 4 July. A tough game was allowed to flow by excellent refereeing from Brazilian official Jose Ramiz Wright. England dominated the match up until the last ten minutes of the first half when the Germans almost scored from a breakaway. After a goalless first period, England again pushed forward but a cruel deflection saw West Germany take the lead in the 59th minute. Awarded a free kick on the edge of Peter Shilton's penalty box, Andy Brehme blasted his shot at the England defenders in the wall. The ball struck England defender Paul Parker and looped over the despairing 'keeper who could only manage to palm the ball into the roof of his net. The game continued, each team cancelling out the other in every department. Lineker equalised for England with ten minutes remaining when he latched onto a Parker cross. Three German defenders panicked and failed to clear the ball and he hit a low left-foot shot across keeper Ilgner to equalise. Both teams could have scored the winner in extra time, Waddle and Buchwald both seeing shots come back off an upright. 1-1 after extra time meant a penalty shoot-out. Matthäus scored with his effort and the teams were level at 2-2 when the normally reliable England fullback Stuart Pearce blasted his effort directly at the 'keeper. After Chris Waddle also failed Germany were through to a record sixth World Cup final and their third consecutive appearance, another record. The match against Argentina was a repeat of the final in Mexico four years previously. The Argentinians, clearly not the team of the mid 1980s, were negative in their approach to the game. Previously, no World Cup final had produced less than three goals, but with the South Americans' negative approach and Germany's hesitance in front of goal, this game looked odds on to do so. The rules dictate, because of the penalty shoot-out, that a team can lift the World Cup without winning a single game throughout the competition. It seemed for a long time that Argentina were prepared to do this. The game was one of the worst ever in the history of the tournament, a complete contrast to four years previously. The Argentinians seemed to sense that their opponents would overwhelm them should they make any attempt to play attractive football. In the 68th minute substitute Pedro Damian Monzon made history when he became the first player to be dismissed in a World Cup final for a trip on Klinsmann. From that moment Mexican referee Mendez lost control of the game. In the 77th minute Gustavo

Abel Dezotti followed Monzon for an early bath. Maradona and his colleagues surrounded the referee as they pushed and pulled him. Seven minutes from the end of the worst World Cup final ever, Rudi Voller ran onto a through ball and was hauled down in the penalty area by Sensini. Lothar Matthäus, the normal penalty taker handed the ball to Andreas Brehme who scored with ease to give West Germany the World Cup. This was the first time in the history of the final that no goals had been scored from open play. Matthäus said later that he was wearing new boots and didn't feel confident enough to take the spot kick! He became the third West German captain the lift the trophy and was named both West German and European Player of the Year.

Matthäus returned to Bayern at the end of the 1991-2 season, but did not figure in the 1992 European Championships due to injury. Germany

USA 1994. Matthäus of Germany and Carlos Borja of Bolivia walk onto the field before the opening game of the 1994 World Cup at Soldier Field in Chicago, Illinois.

Italy 1990: Germany captain Lothar Matthäus is fouled by Paul Parker of England during the 1990 World Cup semi-final in Rome, Italy

surprisingly lost the final to unfancied Denmark, 2-0. The next season, he was back at his best and Bayern won the Bundesliga title in 1993-94. Serious injury kept him out of the game for several months, before he played his 100th game for his country, by now a united Germany, in the summer of 1993 against England in the United States. By the time the 1994 World Cup came around he was playing sweeper, emulating the great Beckenbauer. He scored to put Germany ahead in the quarter final against Bulgaria, but the team fell to a 2-1 defeat. The Germans responded to their latest 'crisis' by winning the 1996 European Championships at Wembley after going through on penalties against hosts England. Matthäus, however, played no part following an embarrassing public row with team-mate Jurgen Klinsmann over the team captaincy. He helped Bayern secure the UEFA Cup (1996), another Bundesliga title (1996-97) and the German Cup (1998) before being surprisingly called up for the 1998 World Cup finals in France – his fifth such tournament. Past his best but still a formidable

force, Matthäus began on the substitutes' bench. When he came on for Dietmar Hamann against Yugoslavia, he broke the record number of World Cup finals appearances: 22 in all. Returning to the line-up gave him three more and his record now stands at 25. The Germans went out to Croatia in the quarter-final. In 1999, at the age of 37, Lothar Matthäus made his record breaking 144th appearance for his country, albeit in a 2-1 defeat at the hands of bitter rivals Holland. He was also in the Bayern team that lost the European Cup final against Manchester United in Spain. He was named as German 'Player of the Year' before retiring and ending his career in the MSL with the NY/NJ Metro Stars. He was subsequently recalled for the 2000 European Championships and played in all three group games, but the campaign ended in disaster although he reached the personal landmark of 150 caps. He spent the 2001-02 season as coach of Rapid Vienna before being dismissed in May 2002.

KEMPES
QUICKSILVER

MARIO KEMPES

ARGENTINA

Mario Alberto Kempes was born on 15 July 1954 in Bell Ville, Cordoba, Argentina. His father had chosen not to be a professional footballer as a young man when playing for local side Leones. Mario, however, had other ideas. Nicknamed 'El Matador' Kempes was a player with amazing close ball skills. He would effortlessly glide past one player then the next, his runs always swift and direct, moving like quicksilver into the heart of the opposition defence. This might suggest that he was a selfish individual, but nothing could be further from the truth - he was the perfect team player. He began his senior career with Instituto Cordoba before moving on to Rosario Central where he scored 100 goals in a little over two years with the club. He won his first cap against Bolivia in September 1973 and never looked back. He was transferred to Valencia of Spain in 1976. In his first season with the Spanish club, he was top scorer with 24 goals, the highest total in the Primera Liga for ten years and the following season he added a further 28 goals. Honours followed and Valencia won the Copa del Rey in 1979 and went on to defeat Arsenal on penalties to take the European Cup Winners' Cup 12 months later. In March the following year, River Plate of Argentina paid £1 million to secure his talents.

Mario Kempes' World Cup career began in the qualifying games in September 1973 as Argentina kicked off with a 4-0 win against Bolivia. The team eventually topped their South American group and qualified for the finals in Germany, dropping only one point along the way. They then found themselves pitted against Italy, Haiti and Poland in their opening group. The Argentinian side played well but lost their first game against Poland 3-2 in the Neckar Stadium in Stuttgart. The Poles went two goals ahead after only eight minutes after Kempes missed an early chance. In the 62nd minute, Atletico Madrid's Ruben Ayala sent Kempes through the Polish defence, and he then passed to Heredia, who pulled one back for South Americans. Two minutes later, Lato, destroyer of England in the qualifiers, scored Poland's third before Babbington netted another for Argentina five minutes from time. The next game saw Italy playing against Argentina. Kempes was ineffective for most of the match and indeed both teams seemed satisfied with a 1-1 draw. Although Argentina deserved to win the game was played at such a slow pace, that each side rarely

Argentina 1978. Mario Kempes makes his way through the Netherland's midfield in the final.

threatened the other. The defeat against Poland and the draw against Italy meant that they had to win their final game against Haiti to stay in the competition. Though they scored four they barely made it, that final goal sending them through to the second phase at Italy's expense. Argentina moved into the second phase group with old rivals Brazil and favourites Holland. East Germany, appearing in their first World Cup made up the group. In their first game they were hammered 4-0 by Holland and then faced equally tough opponents in tbhe shape of Brazil. Although the scores were even at half time, Brazil ran out comfortable winners despite the 2-1 score line. Brazil fielded Jairzinho and Rivelino, winners in 1970, and they scored the goals that beat their South American rivals. Kempes was mostly ineffective again and was substituted late in the game by Houseman. Argentina's final game in the 1974 competition was against East Germany. Both teams were already out of the tournament and they fought an uninspiring 1-1 draw. Kempes, even though playing in all Argentina's six games, failed to score and was a major disappointment.

Four years later it was a very different story. At 26, Kempes was at the peak of his career in Argentina in 1978. Their chain-smoking coach Cesar Menotti decided to build his team with home based players. However, his decision to

select Kempes, who at that time was playing in Spain with Valencia, was his masterstroke, tempered only by his decision to leave out a blossoming 17-year-old by the name of Diego Maradona. Argentina finished second in their group to Italy, beating France and Hungary 2-1 in both matches before losing their final group game 1-0 to Italy. They moved forward to the second phase where they faced Brazil, Peru and Poland. In the New Rosario Stadium in Rosario, the home nation beat Poland 2-0 before a crowd of 40,000. Kempes scored both goals on one of his old pitches. His return to scoring form could not have come at a better time, as the team's main striker Luque missed the game through injury. His first goal came after 15 minutes, when he powerfully headed home a cross from Bertoni. Kaz Deyna, playing his 100th game for Poland, missed a penalty before Kempes added his second with a drive from 12 yards following good work from Ossie Ardiles. The next game against Brazil was a different story. The South Americans battled out a 0-0 draw with Kempes appearing out of position in midfield. The draw put both nations on course for the final, though to reach the final itself, either team would need to top the group. The fact that Argentina played all their games in the evening, knowing exactly the results they needed and that after their opponents had endured the heat of the day, apparently went unnoticed. Brazil beat

Argentina 1978. Kempes takes a well earned rest in the Group B match against Brazil.

Argentina 1978. Kempes celebrates a goal in the final against the Netherlands.

Poland 3-1 in their final group match, leaving Argentina to win their last game by at least three goals. Argentina faced Peru and hammered them 6-0. It was widely noted that the Peruvian goalkeeper, Quiroga, had been born in Argentina. Kempes scored two more as did team-mate Luque with Tarantini and Houseman completing the scoring as Argentina marched into the final against Holland, their first appearance at this stage since 1930. The match was held in Buenos Aires on the 25 June 1978 in front of 77,260 spectators. A touch of professionalism crept into the game before a ball was kicked as Argentina

kept the Dutch team waiting for five minutes and then complained about a light plaster cast worn by Rene van de Kerkhof. The game eventually started ten minutes late. Kempes opened the scoring in the 38th minute following approach work by Luque and Ardiles. In a closely contested match Dutch substitute Dick Nanninga scored the equaliser with a header from a deep cross by van de Kerkhof. With the game moving towards extra time Holland had the Argentinians on the run. With two minutes to go, Rob Resenbrink shot against the post. Their chance had gone. In the final minute of the first period of extra time, Kempes struck again, scoring his sixth goal of the tournament after beating three Dutch defenders to toe poke the ball home. Five minutes from the end, midfielder Daniel Bertoni scored the last goal for Argentina after Kempes had again opened up the Dutch defence. Holland's 'Total Football' had been defeated at the final hurdle for the second time in four years and one has to wonder if Dutch maestro Johan Cruyff had decided to play in these finals could they have beaten Argentina? We will never know and the victory and celebration belonged with the South Americans. Argentina were world champions for the first time in their history. On the downside, there was much speculation of bribery and allegations that Peru allowed Argentina to beat them to oust Brazil from the tournament. Whatever the case, the result stood and Kempes, leading goal-scorer in the 1978 finals, played a major part in bringing the World Cup to Argentina and was voted player of the tournament.

1980 saw Kempes move back to his home country and River Plate and he scored the goal that secured them the national title ahead of Boca Juniors, Maradona and all. The devaluation of the Argentinian currency meant that River Plate could no longer pay Kempes his salary and he returned to Spain, signing for Valencia once more. Four years later, Argentina came to Spain for the 12th World Cup as an older, if not wiser team. The first game saw no less than nine of the previous World Cup winning side take the field against Belgium. Maradona had been added to the side and, age apart, the Argentinians looked quite formidable. The first ten minutes belonged solely to the South Americans as they battered at the Belgian defence. After this display, their frustration set in and the Argentinian defence let in Belgian striker Vandenbergh to score the winner after an hour. Kempes was again out of touch as Argentina stumbled at the first hurdle. In the second game Hungary were hammered 4-1, with Maradona scoring twice. The Argentinians, now believed they could retain their title. A 2-0 win over El Salvador put them into the second phase. However they suffered a near collapse at this stage, with defeats against Italy, 2-1, and an embarrassing display against Brazil, when their rivals humiliated them with a fine performance despite only winning 3-1. Kempes was taken off and replaced by Diaz late in the game after another disappointing performance. His World Cup career was now at an end after 18 matches, only three less than the record.

Argentina 1978. Kempes in the Group B match against Brazil.

Argentina 1978. Kempes is followed closely in the Group One match against France.

His fabulous career waned following the finals in Spain. Kempes moved to another Spanish side, Hercules for whom he scored the winner in the Bernabeau Stadium, home to the mighty Real Madrid. A period in Austria with Vienna and Austria Salzburg came next before he again returned to Spain. In 1995 he returned to Argentina to head the Provincial School of Football with former team-mate Leopoldo Luque. A year later, he was appointed coach of Indonesia and in 1997 became coach of Albania. Political unrest saw Kempes leave that post since then he has been working for Argentinian TV and coached the top Bolivian team, The Strongest.

RIVELINO
THE BANDIT

ROBERTO RIVELINO

BRAZIL

With his small, compact body, muscular thighs and Mexican bandit-style moustache, Rivelino looked more than an extra from a spaghetti western than a world class international footballer. The only doubt about his overall fitness was his lack of stamina, though he more than made up for this with his tremendous skill. Roberto Rivelino was born in Sao Paulo, Brazil on 1 January 1946 and made his name with the Corinthians club. He won his first cap as a 22-year-old against Mexico in 1968, scoring on his debut despite his team suffering a 2-1 defeat.

By 1970, with Rivelino playing to his true potential, Brazilian coach Zagallo had a major problem. His squad was blessed with probably the two best left-footed attacking players in the world and the problem was which one would play in the vital left-sided midfield role. Gerson, older and wiser than Rivelino, could not possibly be omitted from the team. Zagallo solved his problem the easy way – he played them both. Rivelino relished his new deep-lying position that left him free to break with a forward line of Tostao, Jairzinho and the brilliant Pelé. Moreover, he would not need the stamina that was needed to play effectively in midfield. He was a true revelation in the 1970 World Cup finals. In the opening fixture against Czechoslovakia, the Europeans had taken a shock early lead through the swift running of striker Petras. Then in the 24th minute Brazil were awarded a free kick. Jairzinho placed himself in the Czech wall to the astonishment of the defending team. All eyes were on Pelé and Gerson, both masters of the dead ball situation. However, both broke wide to let in Rivelino who delivered a left-foot shot. Jairzinho dropped like a stone and the ball whistled through the gap he had left and into the back of the net. Brazil went on to crush the Czechs 4-1. In the second group game against holders England, Rivelino had to play left midfield because Gerson had picked up an injury in the first game. He played well in the role, although he had to restrict some of his natural instincts. Brazil won the clash of the giants 1-0 with a goal from Jairzinho. Rivelino himself picked up a slight injury in the England game and Paulo Cesar replaced him in the final group game against Romania. The 3-2 final score line flattered the Europeans and Brazil coasted through to the quarter-finals. Both Rivelino and Gerson returned from injury to face a Peruvian side coached by former Brazil favourite Didi. Rivelino scored the

Germany 1974. Rivelino in action in the Group Two match against Yugoslavia.

first goal after only 11 minutes with a stinging left-foot shot that swerved as it hugged the ground before beating the keeper. Four minutes later he passed the ball to striker Tostao to hit the first of his two goals. Although the Peruvians kept plugging away at their opponents' defence, the men from Rio were never in serious trouble. Jairzinho completed the scoring and Brazil ran out 4-2 winners in front of a 54,000 crowd. The semi-final saw them pitched against two times World Cup winners Uruguay. Playing the game in the Jalisco Stadium, Guadalajara, the venue of all their previous matches, gave the Brazilians an advantage. They also sought revenge for their defeat 20 years earlier by the Uruguayans in a game that decided the destiny of the trophy. This time, however, there would be no upsets, despite the Brazilians looking out of touch in the opening minutes of the game. Uruguay went ahead in the 19th minute following a shot from Cubilla. Clodoaldo equalised right on half time. In the second half the Brazilians were on top, but only their goalkeeper Felix stopped the Uruguayans going ahead with a world class save from a header from danger man Cubilla. Jairzinho scored to put his team two up before Rivelino smashed home after receiving a pass from Pelé in the last minute. Brazil were in their fourth World Cup final and nothing was going to stop them keeping the Jules Rimet Trophy for ever. The 1970 Final took place on 21 June in the magnificent Azteca Stadium, Mexico City.

International USA Bicentennial 1976. Gerry Francis (R) of England closely marks Rivelino (L) of Brazil.

Germany 1974. Rivelino prepares for the 3rd and 4th World Cup play off against Poland.

Standing between Brazil and victory were the formidable Italians, who had defeated the West Germans 4-3 in the other semi-final. Whoever won this game would keep the Jules Rimet Trophy, as both countries had won it twice before. It was a game of contrasting styles: the attacking flair and skill of the Brazilians against the defensive solidity of the Italians. Still, their opponents could boast of the great Luigi Riva,

Sandro Mazzola and the midfield genius of Gianni Rivera, sadly used only as a substitute in the closing minutes. Brazil went ahead through Pelé who headed home a lob from Rivelino. The flood gates were now, presumably open, but against the run of play, Roberto Boninsegna scored an equaliser eight minutes before half time following a mix up in the Brazilian defence. In the second half with the game poised at 1-1, Gerson took command. In the 65th minute, he shot them into the lead with a stunning left foot shot that whistled past Italian keeper Albertosi. Brazil at last came alive and took the match to the struggling Italians. Five minutes later Jairzinho scored a third and captain Carlos Alberto finished a thrilling move with the fourth from a pass from the irrepressible Pelé. Roberto Rivelino, although not getting on the score sheet in the final, played a magnificent part in his country's World Cup win. When he appeared in the finals again four years later, he would be a lone shining star in a fading Brazilian cluster.

In the 1974 tournament, held in West Germany, Rivelino wore the famous number ten shirt and was by now captain. At last playing in central midfield, he could only wish for the support he had had in the shape of Pelé, Tostao, Gerson and Clodoaldo four years previously. This Brazilian side lacked the flair of its predecessors and the team was going through what can best be described as a transitional period. Tired of being kicked around, a degree of steel and determination had been added to the beautiful football they were renowned for. Although Jairzinho, now known simply as 'Jair', was in the team, their first game was a disappointing 0-0 draw against Yugoslavia, who could count themselves unlucky not to have won. Rivelino came closest for Brazil, but the game was a defensive exercise, the sole purpose of both being to avoid defeat. The crowds booed the two sides, especially the Brazilians, who were clearly not interested in moving forward in an effort to win the game. Five days later Brazil faced Scotland, in the finals for the first time since 1958. The South Americans were the better team in the first half, Rivelino leading from midfield, but the Scots held out. In the second half, Brazil faded and Scotland were unlucky not to score through Bremner, Lorimer and Jordan. In the final group game, Brazil needed to beat minnows Zaire by three clear goals to move into the second phase. Jairzinho scored the first in the 12th minute and they dominated from then on. They had to wait until the 59th minute for a scorching left footer from Rivelino which almost burst the Zaire net and 11 minutes from time Valdomiro's weak shot seemed to be covered by the goalkeeper, but he let the effort slip past him into the net. Brazil were through and Scotland returned home undefeated yet out of the

honour of the first goal went to Rivelino. Surrounded by three Argentinian defenders, he let fly a left-foot screamer into the net after 31 minutes. Brindisi equalised only 3 minutes later with a neat free kick but after the break Jair scored the winner with a header from Ze

Germany 1974. Rivelino is brought to the ground in the Group Two match against Yugoslavia.

competition. They next came up against East Germany in the first match of the second phase and at least on this occasion there were glimpses of the old flair. Rivelino scored the only goal in a closely contested game. As in Mexico, Jairzinho placed himself in a defensive wall after Brazil were awarded a free kick. As he fell out of the way, Rivelino drove the ball past the 'keeper and into the net. Brazil now faced old rivals Argentina in the next game and ran out 2-1 winners in a match they dominated, despite the closeness of the score line. It was the first meeting of the countries in the World Cup finals and the

Maria's cross. If Brazil could overcome the masterful Dutch team, boasting Cruyff and Neeskens, in the final game of this phase, they would be in the final yet again. Holland were playing their 'Total Football' with Cruyff the best player in the world and some of his team-mates not far behind him in the reckoning. Brazil needed to win, while Holland only needed a draw. Brazil were clearly in awe of the magnificent Dutchmen and began the game with a series of ferocious tackles that left everyone wondering what had happened to the magic of years before. Holland gave as good as they got, but were clearly provoked. The first half ended goalless. The Brazilians now had 45 minutes to come out of their defensive shells and attack the Europeans if they wanted to appear in the final. After 50 minutes Cruyff and Neeskens started and finished a move that saw Neeskens chip the ball over goalkeeper Leao's head. Rivelino rallied his team and it was only now, with the possibility of defeat looming fast, that Brazil began to play, but it was too late. Johann Cruyff volleyed home a perfect cross from Ruud Kroll and the Brazilians were all but out. Six minutes before time defender Luis Pereira was sent off for an appalling tackle on Johann Neeskens. Five of his team-mates were booked but Brazil had lost their crown and their 25-year reputation in a single 90-minute spell.

Rivelino left his old club Corinthians for Fluminense of Rio. He played his 100th game for Brazil against West Germany in the United States Bi-Centennial Tournament in 1976. In the 1978 World Cup finals in Argentina Rivelino, now aged 32, was the only surviving player from 1970 and the cornerstone of another disappointing Brazilian side that failed to impress. In their first group match against Sweden, he had a poor game. The Swedes took the lead in the 37th minute before Reinaldo equalised in injury time of the first half. Brazilian coach Claudio Coutinho dropped his skipper from the second game after he had publicly voiced his disagreements with his boss. Brazil struggled to a 0-0 draw. In their third group match they faced a strong Austrian side, already assured of a place in the second phase. Rivelino was still not selected and Zico, one of Brazil's finest ever players did not appear until the final ten minutes, coming on to replace Mendonca. Roberto scored the only goal of the

game for Brazil in the 40th minute. It was another depressing display from the Brazilians, who still found themselves in the second phase. Again, if they wanted to reach the final, they would have to get some kind of shape to their team. They found themselves in Group B along with Peru, Poland and Argentina. In the first game, against Peru, Brazilian manager Coutinho found himself under a good deal of pressure to get his line-up right. Despite his problems, he still refused to play Rivelino and disgruntled Brazilian fans burned effigies of the coach in an effort to get their star player back in the team. Brazil pushed Peru aside in their best performance for many years, running out 3-0 winners. Dirceu, the man keeping Rivelino out of the team, did his claim no harm bending in a 22-yard free kick in the 14th minute. Dirceu scored again and later substitute Zico netted from the penalty spot to give the Brazilians a resounding victory. In the next game against Argentina the two teams played out a gruelling 0-0 draw which suited them both. Brazil needed to win their last match against Poland and by as many goals they could. Again Rivelino was not in the starting line and only appeared later as a substitute. Brazil won 3-1, but did not appear in the final due to Argentina winning their game against Peru by 6-0. Roberto Rivelino's final game in the World Cup finals came in the third-place playoff against Italy. He appeared as a substitute for the injured Cerezo and had a hand in the second Brazilian goal. His cross was chested down by Mendonca for Dirceu to volley into the net from 20 yards and give Brazil a 2-1 win. They left Argentina for home unbeaten in the tournament. The great Rivelino never played for Brazil again and one can only wonder what might have happened if he had played in all their games.

ZICO
THE WHITE PELÉ

ZICO
BRAZIL

Born Arthur Coimbra Antunes in Brazil on 3 March 1953, Zico attracted attention as a 13-year-old playing indoor football. The team doctor of Flamengo, one of Brazil's top sides, spotted the teenager and was impressed with his skill on the ball and his movement off it. They signed him up and began to nurture his immense talent. He eventually developed into a centre forward before moving back into midfield later in his career. Although dogged by injuries, Zico was almost as good as Pelé, but not quite. Nevertheless he was a truly gifted player, and one of the greats of the Brazilian game. Although he did not win a regular place in the Flamengo line-up until he was 20, it was not long before his skills were recognised all around the soccer world. In 1976 he scored 63 goals in 70 games for Flamengo, an incredible feat; the following season he netted no less than 48 in 56 games. Zico made his full international debut at the age of 23 against rivals Argentina, scoring in a 2-1 win from the type of free kick that he later became famous for. He was 'South American Footballer of the Year' three times (1977, 1981 and 1982) and played a career total of 1,047 senior games. He won four championship medals and scored 650 goals with Flamengo before transferring to Udinese of Italy in 1983.

Brazil were again amongst the favourites to win the World Cup in Argentina in 1978. They had at last shaken off their defensive reputation that had dogged them in the period after the great Pelé retired and returned to what they did best: play simple football with style and panache. To the disappointment of their fans the world over, a disallowed goal by Zico robbed Brazil of victory in their opening game against Sweden. Had this goal counted it would have given them a 2-1 victory and they would have avoided Argentina in the next round by topping their group. Before their next game against Spain captain Roberto Rivelino fell into dispute with the team coach and was promptly dropped. Brazil only managed a dismal 0-0 draw and they were lucky to achieve that as Spanish forward Cardonosa failed to put away a simple chance. Zico did not finish the game after being injured in a tackle and he was replaced by Mendonca. In the third and final group game against Austria, he only made the substitutes' bench. Needing a win to progress to the next phase, Brazil scored the only goal of the game through Roberto. A frustrated Zico replaced Mendonca seven

Spain 1982. Zico in action in the Group C match with Argentina.

minutes from time and had little chance to get into the game, never mind show his talents. He finally got his name on the score sheet in the 3-0 thrashing of Peru in their first Group B game. Coming on a substitute for Gil, Zico converted a 70th minute penalty. The game showed Brazil at their best and people at last began to talk of them as possible winners again. Argentina were next and Zico was only named as substitute again. This 0-0 draw suited both teams and Zico made his appearance late in the game, again replacing the in form Mendonca. The goalless draw meant that one of these teams would be appearing in the final three days away. But which one? Much controversy has surrounded the later stages of the 1978 World Cup. Arch rivals Argentina played their games in the evening when it was cooler and always after Brazil had played their matches. In the final group game, Zico played from the start of the match only to be replaced by Mendonca late in the game. Brazil did, however, beat Poland 3-1 with goals from Nelinho and two from Roberto. This result meant that the Argentinians knew what they had to do to qualify for the final. Stories of bribery and corruption surround the match. Argentina ran out 6-0 winners over Peru and topped the group, qualifying for the final on goal difference. Zico did not make an appearance in the third-place playoff. It was a disappointing end to the

1978 World Cup for both Zico and Brazil, a tournament they felt they could, and maybe should, have won.

In 1981 he scored the only goal of the game against England at Wembley, leaving a stunned Ray Clemence wondering how he had bent the ball around him from so far out. A master of free kicks, body swerves and the killing pass, Zico was at his best aged 29 in the 1982 World Cup tournament held in Spain when Brazil, along with a new coach in Tele Santana and the old attacking style, were favourites to win their fourth World Cup. Zico scored a hat-trick against Bolivia in the qualifying rounds to ensure Brazil's place in the finals as they qualified in style, winning all four games and scoring 11 goals in the process. Their squad was regarded as the best since Pelé's time, 12 years before and they had high hopes of victory. In their first group game they faced a talented Soviet side. Bal scored first for their opponents and they took this lead into half time. The game was played to the constant beat of the Samba with tremendous skill shown from both teams. Brazil looked beaten despite their attacking style, but had the Soviets on the ropes on more than one occasion. It was left to their captain and newest sensation, the bearded Socrates, to equalise with a brilliant goal with only 15 minutes remaining.

He sidestepped two defenders before unleashing an unstoppable shot from outside the penalty area. Brazil scored the winner two minutes from time through Eder, leaving a stunned Soviet team with nothing for their tremendous contribution to a great game of football. The next game saw Brazil face Scotland. The Brazilians outplayed the gallant Scots from the kick off and despite going a goal behind from a magnificent shot from

time when midfielder Falcao netted with a scorching 25-yard effort. Scotland had been heavily defeated with little consolation from the fact that no team in the competition would have lived with the Brazilians that night. No hopers New Zealand were next on the pitch with Brazil and were swept away by 4-0. In the biggest game of their footballing history, the Kiwis could only marvel at Brazil's superiority. Zico scored

Spain 1982. Zico (R) takes on Argentina's Daniel Passerella (L) with Maradona looking on in the background in their Group C encounter.

defender David Narey took the game 4-1. In the 33rd minute, Zico stepped up and scored the equaliser with a brilliant free kick, bending the ball around the Scottish wall, leaving goalkeeper Alan Rough watching in admiration as the ball dropped into his net. In the second half the game belonged to Brazil and it was only a matter of time before they took the lead. Defender Oscar headed home a cross from full back Junior before a glorious chip from winger Eder put the South Americans well and truly in the driving spot. Brazil sealed the game four minutes from

the first of the four with a spectacular bicycle kick in the 29th minute when he latched onto a cross from Leandro. Two minutes later Leandro again crossed for Zico, 'the new Pelé', to powerfully shoot his and Brazil's second. After the break the only interest was how many would Brazil score. Zico, playing one his best games for his country, passed to Falcao in the 55th minute for the midfielder to drive home a third. In the 70th minute, the game all but won, Zico again let in Serginho to fire in the fourth. Surely no one could stop the mighty Brazilians? They entered

Spain 1982. Zico celebrates scoring the opening goal with a spectacular overhead kick in the Group Six match against New Zealand.

the next phase with their heads high. Seemingly invincible, they again met up with their old rivals Argentina. The holders were out of sorts throughout this tournament and many of the winning side, sadly by now past their best, were still in the team. A young Maradona had his final chance to stamp his undoubted skill on the tournament, but after a frustrating and disappointing performance he was sent off in the final minutes after kicking Batista in the groin. Brazil were far superior to Argentina and their game showed the gulf between the two sides. Zico scored the first goal after a free kick from

Eder came back off the crossbar. No Argentinian defenders were near the ball. The Brazilians dominated the match and it was surprising that their second goal came as late as the 67th minute. Centre forward Serginho scored with a header from a Falcao cross to put them two goals up. The best goal of the game was scored by full back Junior when he tapped the ball in following a dazzling five-man move. Diaz pulled one back for Argentina in the last minute, but his goal was not even a consolation. The final second phase game brought Italy and Brazil together. Brazil only needed a draw for an appearance in the final, while Italy had to win. Paulo Rossi, back in the Italian team following a two-year ban, had been quiet prior to this game. He scored his first goal of the competition after only five minutes. The Brazilian defence was caught sleeping when Carbrini found the head of Rossi with his deep cross. Brazil seemed untroubled, they had come back from a goal down against the Soviet Union and Scotland and it was surely only a matter of time before they took the lead. Italy and Rossi had other ideas. In the 11th minute, Serginho missed the easiest chance of the game a minute before Socrates equalised from the narrowest of angles to score his second goal of the tournament. Zico, tightly marked by Italian hard man Claudio Gentile, was finding life difficult. Rossi put Italy ahead in the 25th minute

way through the second period. The Brazilians were on top and pressurising Zoff's goal, but they paid the price for their all out attacking style. Pushing ever forward for the winner, they allowed Italy to break and Rossi completed his hat-trick after Junior weakly headed away a corner. The Brazilians almost scored in the dying minutes when the ball seemed to cross the line. The referee decided against it and Brazil, the favourites and the best team in the competition, were out.

In 1983, at the age of 30 and after playing all his domestic football in Brazil, Zico left Flamingo for the lure of the lire and signed for one of the less glamorous sides in Serie A, Udinese. He filled the stadium week after week, his silky skills

France 1998. Brazil coaches Mario Zagallo (L) and Zico (R) before the Group A encounter with Morocco.

following a glaring mistake by the Brazilian defence. Italy then missed two more chances to make the game safe but failed to capitalize on their superiority. Falcao, suddenly finding a clear sight of goal, thundered in a 20-yard shot half

appreciated by the soccer-crazed Italians. They soon took him to their hearts. In his first season, he scored 19 goals in 24 games; even the ruthless marking of the Italian defenders could not stop him. Midway through the following season however, another side to Zico became apparent. Again hampered by injury and amid tax fraud allegations, he returned to Brazil and rejoined Flamengo. He later led a campaign to stamp out the brutal marking in the Brazilian league after being badly hurt in one game. In the 1986 Mexico World Cup, a clearly unfit Zico came on as a substitute against France in the quarter-final and missed a vital penalty minutes before full time. Brazil went out of the competition via a penalty shoot-out after the sides could not break the stalemate during extra time. Although a great player boasting sublime skills, Zico did not achieve the dazzling heights of those other Brazilian stars of the early 1970s. The will and skill were obviously there, but with the great pressure to emulate the success of his heroes plus the increasing time spent injured, one has to feel that somehow Zico was a talent unfulfilled. In all he played 78 games for Brazil and scored 54 goals. He retired in 1990 and was later appointed Brazil's Minister of Sport. In 1994 he and former World Cup winner Mario Zagallo were technical advisors to coach Carlos Alberto Perreiro as Brazil won their fourth World Cup.

GULLIT
THE RASTAMAN

RUUD GULLIT

NETHERLANDS

Despite being an immensely talented player Ruud Gullit only played in one World Cup final tournament. After being one of the top nations of the 1970s and reaching the final in both 1974 and 1978, the team went into a near terminal decline and failed to qualify for the 1982 and 1986 finals. Emerging as a footballing force once again in 1988 they went on to win the European Championship, knocking out England along the way. Holland began to field a team capable of playing the kind of football the 1970s team was renowned for. When AC Milan approached Dutch champions PSV Eindhoven, they left with PSV's star player, Ruud Gullit in return for a cheque for £5.7m pounds. The arrival of Gullit and his international colleague Marco van Basten signalled the end of the Milan careers of two English imports Ray Wilkins and Mark Hateley. Although barely out of his teens when he first appeared on the international scene in 1983, it was not until he produced a stunning display in the 2-2 draw at Wembley against England in 1988 that he really established himself. That summer, Gullit and Van Basten blew everyone aside, powering the Dutch team to glory in the European Championships. Gullit, dreadlocks spraying wildly, scored with a bullet header in the final. Van Basten scored the other after gloriously volleying past the Soviet goalkeeper from a deep cross from Arnold Muhren.

The eyes of the football world were on the Dutch as the World Cup drew nearer and Gullit became Holland's key player as their assault on Italia '90 began. Then, after an injury, Gullit's right knee became suspect and it was rumoured time and time again that not only would he miss the finals, but he might never play again. Absent for almost an entire season for Milan, Gullit returned for the European Cup final gloriously scoring two against Steau Bucharest, before being substituted. After two more operations he went back into full training, proved his fitness and rightfully regained his place in the Dutch national side. Gullit and his knee marched defiantly on to Italy. The Dutch won their qualifying group by one point and were unbeaten. Squabbling in the camp had previously been their biggest flaw – many of the team from the 1970s fought for money off the pitch as hard as they fought for the ball on it. Following coach Rinus Michels' exodus after the 1988 European championships, new coach Thijs Libregts was in the hot seat. Later, the Dutch players would fight against the

1988 European Championships. Ireland goalkeeper Pat bonner (right) punches clear from Ruud Gullit with a little help from teammate Mick McCarthy.

coach, many of them unable to turn out for their country because they felt the team tactics were wrong – they wanted to play the fluid 'Total Football' they were renowned for and which had taken them to two World Cup finals. The players wanted the legendary Johan Cruyff as team coach. Cruyff, his love affair with Spanish giants Barcelona waning, simply wasn't interested. Despite the sacking of Thijs Libregts just before the tournament began, Holland were the favourites to win their first round group despite being paired with England and, with players of

1988 European Championships. Ruud Gullit celebrates as the Netherlands defeat the USSR in the Euro '88 Final. Holland are the new Champions of Europe!

the calibre of Gullit, van Basten and Ronald Koeman, were threatening to dominate the tournament. The other teams in the group, Egypt and the Republic of Ireland both had gifted players but were unlikely to cause any real upsets. Gullit was deemed the second best player in the competition after Argentina's Diego Maradona and for most teams, a half-fit player of Gullit's talents would be enough. However in truth his performances were largely disappointing. The Dutch side, still reeling from off-the-pitch problems were no match for a superior English side. Only rarely did Gullit show his true form and England 'keeper Shilton was never really tested by him. Although inferior in the match, the Dutch managed to pull off a 0-0 draw, despite England's Stuart Pearce and Gary Lineker having efforts disallowed. Gullit finally got himself on the World Cup score sheet against the Republic of Ireland in the last group game, when he netted from the inside right channel in the 10th minute. From a Koeman free kick, he played a sweet one-two with Kieft before striking

an unstoppable shot past Irish 'keeper Bonner. Niall Quinn cut the Dutch celebrations short in the 70th minute when he thumped home the equaliser. England won the group with Holland and the Republic of Ireland coming joint second to move into the second round. Waiting for the Dutch were their old enemies, West Germany, favourites to win the competition. The game turned out to be one of the best of the tournament. In the first 15 minutes Winter missed two gilt-edged chances to put the Dutch ahead and in the 20th minute Frank Rijkaard was booked for a desperate foul on German forward Rudi Voller. Voller complained to the referee that the Dutchman had spat at him. Millions of watching football fans had to agree. The only action the Argentinian referee took was to book the unfortunate Voller and then tell the German to get on with the game. A minute later Voller appeared to kick the Dutch goalkeeper's legs from under him. Van Breukelen fell to the ground and held his leg in agony. The view from a different angle proved without doubt that Voller

Italy 1990. Gullit waves to the crowd as he leaves the pitch after the World Cup second round match with West Germany.

was not guilty of kicking the goalkeeper and had not even made an attempt to do so. Rijkaard joined in the row, pushing and shouting at the German striker. Voller looked bewildered as he

was sent off. Rijkaard was also ordered off and again spat at the innocent Voller as he ran past him off the field. The football resumed and in the 38th minute Pierre Littbarski had a glorious

1988 European Championships. (left to right) Ruud Gullit lifts the European Championship Trophy with Jan Woulters.

chance to give Germany the lead, but van Breukelen made a tremendous save to deny him. After the break, Jurgen Klinsman scored the first goal after a cross from Buchwald. Klinsman then rattled the Dutch post in the 75th minute. Full back Andy Brehme then curled a delightful shot around the Dutch keeper to give the Germans a two-goal advantage. Later in the game the Dutch were lucky to be awarded a penalty after van Basten dived in the penalty area. Ronald Koeman stepped up to cut back the German lead, but it was too late to stop the Germans going through to the semi-final against England. Holland faded along with their brightest star and left the field dejected and well beaten, only two years after they had collected the European Championship trophy in style, ironically on German soil.

Following the World Cup in Italy, Gullit's fortunes waxed and waned with Milan. He was transferred to Sampdoria then back to Milan,

stayed a month and then moved back to Sampdoria. His love affair with Italy over, he signed for Glenn Hoddle's Chelsea in 1994 and then became player-manager when Hoddle left to become England coach. He brought a sense of style both on and off the pitch. After taking Chelsea to the FA Cup semi-finals in 1996 (they lost 2-1 to Manchester United, Gullit scoring Chelsea's goal), his team again assaulted the FA Cup and a year later won the final against Middlesborough 3-0. Gullit's stay at Stamford Bridge ended acrimoniously and he left his position at Chelsea under a cloud, but it wasn't long before he found himself back at the helm of a top English club, this time in the north east of England at Newcastle United. Following the departure of Kenny Dalglish, Gullitt's appointment was heralded with almost as much elation as that of Kevin Keegan several years before, and the hope that was lost under Kenny Dalglish's direction was restored, if only for a short while. Gullit took a period to assess the playing squad he had inherited before ousting several established international players. Newcastle reached the F.A. Cup final for the second year running but were out played by a treble-hunting Manchester United and went down 2-0. Reaching Wembley and Europe was a huge bonus, but still the disappointment of the fans hung in the air. Gullitt was by now feeling the pressure and, as the new season began, it was clear that his position was in jeopardy. By the time the meeting with newly promoted rivals Sunderland took place Newcastle's camp was in turmoil. Results were poor and the Magpies

were at the wrong end of the Premiership table. Dressing-room unrest reached a crescendo when Gullit dropped two Tyneside favourites, England captain Alan Shearer and Duncan Ferguson, to the substitutes' bench. Former England midfield star Rob Lee was left to watch games from the stand, humiliated by the fact that he was not even given a first-team squad number. The controversial defeat by Sunderland proved to be the Dutchman's last game in charge of the Tynesiders. He quickly departed and, to date, his football career in England was over.

1996 FA Cup Semi-final. Ruud Gullit of Chelsea takes on Manchester United's Roy Keane.